Marketing in Web 3.0

Marketing in Web 3.0

*Artificial intelligence, the metaverse
and the future of marketing*

Simon Kingsnorth

KoganPage

First published in Great Britain and the United States in 2024 by Kogan Page Limited

2nd Floor, 45 Gee Street
London
EC1V 3RS
United Kingdom

8 W 38th Street, Suite 902
New York, NY 10018
USA

www.koganpage.com

Kogan Page books are printed on paper from sustainable forests.

© Simon Kingsnorth 2024

ISBNs

Hardback   978 1 3986 1555 7
Paperback   978 1 3986 1550 2
Ebook   978 1 3986 1554 0

British Library Cataloguing-in-Publication Data

A CIP record for this book is available from the British Library.

Library of Congress Cataloging-in-Publication Data

Names: Kingsnorth, Simon, author.
Title: Marketing in web 3.0 : artificial intelligence, the metaverse and the future of marketing / Simon Kingsnorth.
Description: London ; New York, NY : Kogan Page, 2024. | Includes bibliographical references and index.
Identifiers: LCCN 2024024900 | ISBN 9781398615502 (paperback) | ISBN 9781398615557 (hardback)
Subjects: LCSH: Marketing. | Artificial intelligence.
Classification: LCC HF5415 .K5225 2024 | DDC 658.8/72028563–dc23/eng/20240716
LC record available at https://lccn.loc.gov/2024024900

Typeset by Integra Software Services, Pondicherry
Print production managed by Jellyfish
Printed and bound by CPI Group (UK) Ltd, Croydon, CR0 4YY

Firstly, a thank you to my supportive wife Ali for doing everything else while I typed away.

Secondly, thanks to Kirsty, who was instrumental in helping me pull this book together.

Thank you to Kogan Page who continue to support my endeavours.

And last, but never least, a big thank you to my wonderful boys, Dexter and Oz, who give me the joy I need to keep me going.

CONTENTS

LIST OF FIGURES

ABOUT THE AUTHOR

 Simon Kingsnorth is a bestselling author and highly experienced marketing leader who has built and led marketing departments for leading brands and consulted to businesses across the world. He is the CEO of SK, a global marketing agency that delivers tailored, strategic marketing solutions to leading brands. He is a keynote speaker on the topics of marketing and the future and is a regular consultant and trainer. He is also a trustee of a number of charities and an advisor to many other businesses.

His first book, *Digital Marketing Strategy*, is an international bestseller and is used by universities and marketing institutes across the world to teach digital marketing. His second, *The Digital Marketing Handbook*, is used by marketing practitioners all over the world and is also used by many universities to teach Masters degrees.

1

The story of digital marketing (so far)

'Those who cannot remember the past are condemned to repeat it.'
GEORGE SANTAYANA, THE LIFE OF REASON, *1905*

When looking ahead to what may be, the wise among us always look back to understand what we have already learned. This saves us from repeating the same mistakes and gets us to the ideal outcome faster. Evolution has been doing this for millennia, and marketers for decades. That's why we start this book with a look at the journey digital marketing has been on in the past 25 years before we get into the detail of what may come in the next 25.

I say 'digital marketing' specifically here because all of what lies ahead will be digital. This is not to say that the principles of marketing that were established long before the word digital was thrown around are invalid. In fact, they are more important than ever. But the key ingredients that paint the backdrop of Web3 are in the digital marketing journey of the late 20th and early 21st centuries.

We will talk much more broadly about marketing in this book than restricting ourselves to digital. In fact, as you will see, Web3 is much more about brand and experience than landing pages and text ads. But let's start with a look at digital marketing in Web1 and Web2.

The history of the World Wide Web (WWW) is a fascinating journey that has transformed the way we communicate, even socialize, gain access to and share information, conduct business and much more. The journey began in the late 1960s with ARPANET, a network of computers at numerous research institutions across the US. However, the WWW as we know it today really began in the 1990s.

In 1990, Tim Berners-Lee, a British computer scientist, invented the WWW while working at CERN. He developed the foundational elements of hypertext, URLs, HTML and HTTP, and from there the release of numerous web browsers such as Mosaic and Netscape Navigator in 1993 (and many more quickly following) made it widely accessible, albeit limited in content at this early stage.

As the content grew, so did the need to be able to find what you wanted from one starting place. Search engines were born and after a short battle for supremacy, Google, founded in 1998, became a clear winner. Initially this was due to the simple quality of the product – the PageRank algorithm. Google focused on what would be a defining principle of many internet businesses over the coming years: simple quality. Where other search engines were trying to feed in news, shopping, chat and more, Google was an empty page with a search bar, but its results were far more accurate and complete than those of its competitors and so users flocked to it, eventually leading Google to become the default verb for searching.

At this time, marketers were just starting to explore what the internet could offer. Early display banners were appearing on news sites and search engine home pages. Businesses were starting to create basic brochureware websites and email marketing was growing at pace.

E-commerce also grew very quickly at this highly entrepreneurial time. Amazon, founded in 1994, was just one of many e-commerce sites that aimed to sell books, CDs and other simple products. But with the development of hyper-personalized recommendations, an enormous catalogue of first-party and third-party products and later super-fast delivery, Amazon became a clear winner. eBay won the race for the auction sites after launching in 1995 and has likewise become a major player among the e-commerce brands.

In the late 1990s search engine optimization (SEO) started to appear as a mysterious and highly scientific discipline. There were those who were trying to create valuable sites that would rank but also those that were trying to game the search engines through techniques such as keyword stuffing and meta tag manipulation. While this 'black hat' approach to SEO still exists today, virtually none of the techniques works anymore. I myself have always believed firmly in the 'white hat' approach and have seen many businesses crash and burn after a quick win using black hat techniques, but it was certainly an interesting time as new technology appeared and people tried to manipulate it for quick gain – something we should all pay close attention to as we move into Web3.

WHITE HAT AND BLACK HAT

Black hat SEO is a term that has been around since the early days of search engine optimization. This technique effectively refers to attempts to try to trick the search engines into giving you preferable results, ultimately exploiting perceived weaknesses in the algorithm. These techniques have yielded very strong short-term results for some businesses, but more often than not ultimately they have caused significant damage to those organizations, including their removal from search engines which I have seen cause millions of dollars of damage and even closure of businesses. Examples include buying thousands of links rather than gaining them organically, putting white text stuffed full of keywords on a white background, gateway pages and much more.

White hat SEO is following the guidance from the search engines to deliver the best outcome for the user and is my strong recommendation. For more detail on this see my book *Digital Marketing Strategy*.

During this time we also saw the introduction of Google Ads. This was the move that transported Google from an impressive search engine to a global superpower. Today Google's annual revenue from its advertising is US$224.47 billion (Statista, 2023). This is 80 per cent of its total annual revenue and so if this income were to disappear, Google as we know it would suffer a significant decline. This is something we'll discuss later in the book as the landscape for search will change dramatically in Web3.

This growth of search engines, explosion of online information and dot com business boom led to the firm establishment of the WWW within just five years from going mainstream – arguably the fastest global technological and cultural revolution in human history. From the early 2000s, the technology advance enabled Web 1.0 to give way to Web 2.0.

Web 2.0 enabled not just static content but interactive functionality and this led to user-generated content (UGC) becoming *the* major source of content on the web. This in turn led to the forums and basic profile-sharing sites such as Friends Reunited and MySpace giving way to rich, engaging social networks such as Facebook and Twitter. Reddit also grew quickly in the mid Noughties and all remain some of the most used sites on the web today.

This led to social media marketing, initially organically and later paid. This has become an enormous industry and one that has driven many tools from analytics to automation. It has also created a phenomenal new source of lead generation which can be highly targeted. However, it has also created many controversies in the use of personal data. The growth in popularity of social media also created the Influencer, which today is a $7.4 billion industry (PR Newswire, 2023).

Consumer behaviour has shifted significantly over this first 30 years of the web too. The convenience of online shopping has disrupted traditional retail – many would say it has in fact seriously harmed it, with many major retail chains going out of business and small independent shops struggling in many areas. Consumers have embraced e-commerce, which means being able to purchase anywhere, any time, and this in turn has reduced patience over delivery times. Social media has given a lot of power to consumers, enabling them to complain publicly to gain compensation and to provide reviews when things go wrong (and right). This gives consumers much more clarity when making a decision, but as with SEO above, has also been open to corruption by the less ethical players.

We have also seen the rise of the Internet of Things (IoT). Security cameras, doorbells, robot vacuums, smart fridges and much more now (fairly) seamlessly integrate with our smart phones and smart watches, with Apple, Amazon and Google largely leading the way. Many of us now control our lights, heating, cleaning, shopping and even cars through smart devices and this opens up a wealth of marketing opportunities. As self-driving vehicles gain mass adoption we can expect in-car marketing opportunities to open up significantly.

Streaming too has enabled us to take ads before traditional television and radio into on-demand music and video through platforms such as Netflix, Amazon Prime, Spotify and many more.

As we move into Web3, as we have seen with Web2, the web is increasingly taking inspiration from sci-fi movies and books – sometimes led by them, sometimes leading them and sometimes coincidentally mirroring them. Franchises such as *Star Trek* with its universal translator, handheld communicators and touch screens; *Star Wars* and its droids, holograms and artificial intelligence; and many more have influenced the technology we use and the technology that many of our engineers and developers are working on creating.

The pace of change here from a marketing industry that was focused on television, radio, press, direct mail, outdoor and other offline channels to one that is immersed in complex data points from thousands of real-time, digital activities across a global audience has been a fascinating journey. But the journey is really just beginning.

When we consider that search engines in 2024 are still simply pages of text links, that emails are still largely the same as they were in 1990, that social media involves trawling through posts you may not be remotely interested in to find those that you are, that advertising sometimes misses the target – it is clear that there are big changes we can make to improve the experience for consumers and marketers alike.

The need for speed

In the past 25 years, the evolution of internet speeds has been nothing short of remarkable. From dial-up connections in the late 1990s to fibre optic networks today, the advancements in technology and, perhaps more impressively, the speed at which the necessary infrastructure has been implemented on a global scale have truly transformed our digital experience.

I'm old enough to remember waiting minutes for a single image to appear on a screen only for the connection to stop and to have to start again because someone in the house picked up the phone when you were trying to use the line for browsing.

Broadband brought a change to all this and so the early 2000s was a time when using the internet became a more pleasant and therefore mainstream experience. We moved from 56 kilobits per second to 256 Kbps and even several megabits per second (Mbps). Now downloading files was easy. Even streaming became possible, which opened the way for video. This led to the launch of YouTube. At this time I recall working on the first ever mobile video campaign in the UK while at Vodafone – something that at the time seemed truly revolutionary.

Fibre optic technology then further advanced the internet landscape by transmitting data through thin strands of glass which progressed speeds to 10 Mbps, 100 Mbps and 1,000 Mbps. This means that speeds can now reach multiple gigabits (see Figure 1.1).

Meanwhile, mobile coverage moved from 2G to 3G through 4G and now to 5G in recent years. This means that while still behind fibre optic standards, mobile devices are more than capable of streaming videos and downloading entire movies in seconds.

This change in speed, alongside improvements in programming, has led to an explosion of web apps. Today, the number of SaaS (software as a service) products available to marketers is in the tens of thousands. Platforms such as HubSpot, Salesforce, Segment, Google Ads, Shopify, Meta Ads, Hootsuite, SurveyMonkey, Mailchimp and many more are available to a digital marketer. These have led to a need to automate and integrate, which in turn has led to a growth of automation platforms (including some of those above). This means that the way a modern marketer works must involve multi-channel campaigns and attribution – an area that many have not yet truly got to grips with and which is certainly not as easy as perhaps it needs to be. The ecosystem

FIGURE 1.1 Global internet speeds 1990–2050

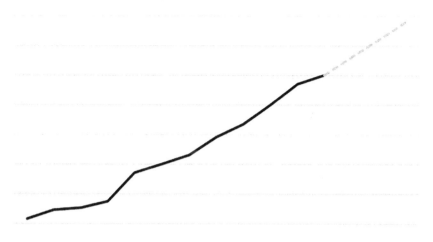

1993 1994 1996 1998 2000 2003 2005 2006 2008 2011 2015 2023 2030 2040 2050

━━━ Speed ⋯ ⋯ ⋯ Forecast

SOURCE Adapted from Future Timeline, 2022

we have created is itself as much of a problem as a solution for many marketers and small business owners – this is something that needs to be addressed in Web3.

Moving into Web 2.5

AI

As I write this in late 2023, artificial intelligence (AI) could not be a hotter topic. Since the start of this year, literally hundreds of AI tools have sprung up to solve a range of problems. Some more successfully than others. Content has been a major area of growth, with generative tools appearing in image, sound, video and more. These can be unreliable and can present unexpected risks, but they are smart tools for the savvy marketer. AI has really hit the mainstream now and many people are quickly repositioning themselves as AI experts to capitalize on this. Many of us therefore see AI as a very 2020s phenomenon.

In reality, the history of artificial intelligence goes back to the Dartmouth Conference in 1956. Early AI research focused on problem-solving before AI went through a period of decline. Machine learning, natural language processing and the IoT have led to a significant acceleration in this and that is what's driving today's headlines and disruptive technology surge.

There are of course both positive and negative connotations for this growth in AI and we'll discuss these later in the book.

The chain gang

Blockchain is another technology that has created widespread disruption over the past 15 years. Blockchain is a digital, decentralized, distributed ledger technology that records and verifies transactions across multiple computers or nodes in a network within a chronological chain of blocks.

That sentence alone is enough to explain why the technology is largely not understood by most people. In fact, there has been more than one example of a cryptocurrency (by definition these are based on blockchain technology) being faked and attracting significant investment despite having no underlying blockchain technology involved – some even simply being run from Excel spreadsheets! In fact, blockchain was invented initially purely to serve as the ledger for Bitcoin, the most popular and established cryptocurrency.

We'll explain more about blockchain later in the book and what impact it may have on marketing, so if none of this makes sense yet, don't worry.

Alongside cryptocurrency and blockchain come NFTs, or non-fungible tokens. You may have seen celebrities, artists and others selling these for significant sums. The question is primarily whether these are a gimmick or a long-term product. We'll explore this later in the book too.

Ready player one

Gaming has grown enormously. It turns out my parents were wrong when they said you couldn't make a career from playing computer games! E-sports has seen enormously in the 2010s and since. There are e-sports for racing, fighting and many more genres across PC, console and even mobile apps.

But why are we talking about gaming in a marketing book? The fact is, whether you love or hate gaming, whether you play, watch or read about it or just avoid it altogether, gaming is here to stay and it brings cultural considerations that marketers need to understand as they build out their Web3 strategy.

We have been talking about and implementing gamification for many years now, using elements of gaming psychology and interfaces to create fun experiences and drive behaviours from our consumers. But Web3 will take this to a whole new level and we'll explore this further later in the book too.

Changing reality

Both augmented reality (AR) and virtual reality (VR) have raised their heads in the past 10–15 years in a meaningful way. VR has been around for decades but it has largely been relegated to movies and sci-fi. Again, we look to *Star Trek* and this time to its Holosuite for inspiration here.

VR has grown significantly with the arrival of mainstream VR headsets that plug in to consoles or even operate stand-alone, such as Meta Quest, Oculus Rift and Playstation VR. VR can already immerse us within popular games and take us on virtual trips around the world, but it is, of course, an important factor as we look forward to the metaverse. We'll discuss what this means and what you need to be thinking about later in the book.

AR meanwhile overlays digital content onto the real world. This can be useful in professional fields such as medicine through weara-bles, but also in entertainment through smart phones, as with *Pokémon GO*. This has a role to play with the metaverse but also for immersive brand experiences and stepping stones to the full VR environment.

So what?

The web so far has brought a lot of change and disruption and I still see us as taking our first steps through the front door – there is a whole building to explore and we don't know our way around it, never mind what is inside, yet.

As we navigate our way through Web 2.5 and into Web3, there is huge potential for brands to make a real mark and reposition themselves for the future, but that also comes with risks. There have been a lot of mistakes made in the journey from 1990 to today as well as a lot of unprecedented successes. In the next chapter we'll look at both of these and understand what went wrong and what we need to ensure we get right in Web3.

Notes

Future Timeline (2022) Global average internet speed, 1990–2050. 25 August, https://futuretimeline.net/data-trends/2050-future-internet-speed-predictions.htm (archived at https://perma.cc/528K-TG9W)

PR Newswire (2023) Influencer marketing platform market size worth 69.92 billion with excellent CAGR of 32.50% by 2029, size, share, industry demand, rising trends and competitive outlook. 23 January, www.prnewswire.co.uk/news-releases/influencer-marketing-platform-market-size-worth-69-92-billion-with-excellent-cagr-of-32-50-by-2029--size-share-industry-demand-rising-trends-and-competitive-outlook-301728149.html#:~:text=Data%20Bridge%20Market%20Research%20analyses,forecast%20period%20of%202022%2D2029 (archived at https://perma.cc/X5FG-7X2E)

PART ONE

The Journey to Web3

2

What have we learned from Web2?

Web2 has been a rollercoaster. It has brought many new experiences to our lives, some for good and other, well, not so much. Brands have had the opportunity to create incredible experiences and run multi-channel, high-impact campaigns with massive reach. Conversely, consumers and businesses have suffered from hacks and trolls and been at the mercy of a limited number of major tech firms. So there have been a lot of issues with Web2 that we need to be mindful of as we go on the journey to Web3.

In this chapter we'll take a look at each of these areas, including what's gone well and perhaps more importantly what hasn't. We'll look at how we can fix, improve and build on these to ensure that the future of the internet for marketers, consumers and brands is a positive experience for all of us.

Privacy

Where else to start but with perhaps the most controversial, widely discussed and regulated issues of the past 25 years. I would also say that this is the most pressing issue and the one that consumers generally feel most passionate about and that is why I want to tackle it in detail before we move on to other areas.

Privacy has been a hot topic for as long as online passwords have existed, but this concern is much wider than authentication or password storage. The past 10 years have seen continuous data leaks. In fact, this has become so common and so accepted that smart phones now report on which of your passwords have been compromised as part of their default software – that itself is quite a statement on the situation. Before we get into the fundamental issues and how to tackle them, let's look at one of the more well-known incidents from recent years.

CASE STUDY

Facebook and Cambridge Analytica

In the mid-2010s, the personal data of millions of Facebook users was collected by Cambridge Analytica (Brown, 2020). This was done predominantly to enable advertising to be highly targeted for an upcoming US election. That in itself is not an issue. As marketers we try to gather data from multiple sources to better understand our audiences and target them effectively. The two biggest issues here however were that this was personal data and it was collected without permission.

The data was collected through an app called 'This Is Your Digital Life', built psychological profiles on users and collected the personal data of their Facebook friends via Facebook's Open Graph platform. The app went on to harvest 87 million Facebook profiles, which Cambridge Analytica then used to assist the Ted Cruz and Donald Trump 2016 presidential campaigns.

Alongside this 'interference' in the US election, Cambridge Analytica was also accused of playing a role in the UK Brexit referendum, although the official investigation did not find any significant breaches.

Christopher Wylie, a former Cambridge Analytica employee, disclosed the above in a series of 2018 interviews with the press and Facebook apologized for its role. However, this was not deemed to be enough and Facebook CEO Mark Zuckerberg was forced to testify in front of the US Congress, with the final outcome being an enormous and unprecedented $5 billion fine for privacy violations.

While this was not the first or only case of psychological targeting, it was both a high-profile case – being concerned with affecting the politics of one of the world's most powerful countries – and a clear case of misuse of personal information. The brand damage to Facebook was extensive enough to cause the hashtag #DeleteFacebook to trend on social media. In fact, following the incident, 74 per cent of Facebook users made some changes to their Facebook usage, from amending privacy settings to taking a break from Facebook to deleting the app or even their profile (Perrin, 2018).

This is a fantastic example of how not to manage data, but it isn't the only one. In fact, it's not even the only one for Facebook. The company also tested alterations to users' feeds to see if certain messages would make people happier or more depressed – a misguided manipulation of people's emotions for the benefit of a scientific experiment. And this is before we discuss data leaks.

In fact, if we look at just 10 data leaks from recent years from the US alone, we can account for more records leaked than the entire population of the world. These leaks have been from companies such as Meta, MySpace, Home Depot, JPMorgan Chase, LinkedIn, Microsoft and many more major firms. Looking at just the year 2018 alone we can see well over 1,000 data leaks in the US, with over 471 million records compromised and 2.2 billion people impacted (Statista, 2023).

These stories (and most of us have one) have brought to the fore the need for tighter regulation and control around personal data and this in turn has led consumers, regulators and politicians to challenge the way companies, and therefore marketers, gather, store and use data. This in turn has led to initiatives such as GDPR in Europe and the California Consumer Privacy Act in the US. Both initiatives were designed to put more rigorous controls in place for protection of data and GDPR especially aimed to ensure that data was not collected through cookies or forms without explicit permission.

These regulations, being political in nature, do not extend globally and are hard to fully enforce, but they did create a shift in the approach that marketers took in targeting. This, combined with the phasing out of third-party cookies in the early 2020s, has created a significant rethink of effective targeting.

While as a marketer it is tempting to gather as much data as possible on an individual and target on every possible factor, I support the move to increased privacy. It is true that knowing your audience better enables you to serve the right ads and get the best outcomes for everyone, but the ownership of personal data lies entirely with the individual and we must accept that we do not have the right to that information unless we are explicitly given that right.

Third-party cookies

For many years, third-party cookies have been a key targeting method for brands to track individual behaviours and serve those individuals with relevant messages in the right place at the right time. However, as we have mentioned already in this book, there have been those that have either abused or poorly executed this opportunity and that has led to a consumer backlash.

One of the key use cases for third-party cookies was to understand what users were doing on our websites and then, when they exited and visited another site, to serve them with advertising to bring them back to our site to convert. This could simply be brand messages, sales offers or could even include the quote they had been given on the site.

This could be highly effective but also was seen as very invasive and, by many consumers, a little creepy. In the last 2010s several

FIGURE 2.1 Share of adults who understood vs did not understand how internet cookies worked in the United States as of October 2022

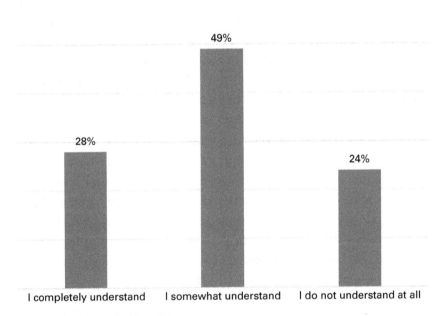

SOURCE Adapted from Statista, 2024

browsers introduced more and more restrictive cookie policies. Of these, Safari was one of the larger names (by user numbers). Google was a little slower to move, with its Chrome browser (over 60 per cent share of the market in October 2021 (Statcounter, 2024)) taking a number of years to phase out third-party cookies following Google's 2020 announcement and with the deadline moving more than once. The tech firms that own these browsers made similar statements. Google, for example, stated in a 2021 blog that it didn't believe solutions such as ad tracking based on personally identifiable information (PII) would meet rising consumer expectations for privacy or evolving regulatory restrictions and made a commitment to preserve privacy while delivering results (Google, 2021).

This is a statement that I felt was very powerful at the time it was made. 'Rising consumer expectations' and 'rapidly evolving regulatory restrictions' are what we have discussed in this chapter and they have been at the forefront of my mind for many years now. As marketers, we need to think smart and play fair as we move from the Web2 'what can I do' way of thinking to the Web3 'what should I do' way of thinking.

Some interesting data on this shift from GetApp and Hubspot (Hubspot, 2022) tells us that:

- 41 per cent of marketers believe their biggest challenge will be their inability to track the right data
- 44 per cent of marketers predict a need to increase their spending by 5 per cent to 25 per cent in order to reach the same goals as 2021
- 23 per cent of marketing experts plan on investing in email marketing software due to Google's new policy

This effectively suggests that marketers are expecting to use other channels more meaningfully and to have to work harder and spend more to target the same people.

As a result of these changes, marketers need to consider how we will tackle these two key challenges. First, how do we build our first-party data? If we cannot use third-party cookies for targeting, how do we gather our own first-party data so that we can use that for accurate targeting? This means creating a value exchange with consumers, ensuring that we can gather the data they are willing to share in exchange for a benefit to them. Perhaps we can consider communities, benefits and hubs that deliver value. This means we can use that data to target those people with the right messages at the right time and with their permission to do so. This reduces consumer irritation and increases marketing effectiveness. After all, is marketing not truly about value exchange?

Second, we need to work smarter. In today's omnichannel world, we need to consider how we reach our audience through the channels that matter to them. We need to truly understand our audience segments and how to truly personalize to them. I discuss what I call True Personalization in my book *Digital Marketing Strategy*. Personalization is not simply about adding someone's name into an email. True Personalization is about talking to that user about what they are interested in, on the channel they prefer, at the time they prefer and with an offer or value-based message that will appeal to them. By understanding our customers and consumers better, we can ensure this is exactly what we deliver – we'll discuss this later in the book.

Mobile app tracking

As Apple launched its iOS operating system update for its devices, it introduced a major new feature. Users could now 'Ask App Not to Track' their activity across other apps and websites. Before this privacy feature was introduced, brands could track users' behaviour through Apple's tools and other third-party platforms. As with third-party cookies, this enabled a strong understanding of consumers' actions and a precise targeting opportunity. However, in 2021 research firm Gartner stated that 85 per cent of people were asking apps not to track them and while it forecasted a drop to 60 per cent by 2023, this remains the majority of users opting out when they could previously be targeted (Gartner, 2021).

Meta objected strongly to this move, stating that it felt it would make targeting harder for ad networks and this would, in turn, harm small businesses. The company even took out full-page newspaper ads to display its frustration at the move. It stated that advertising-based businesses might need to change their entire revenue model, to subscription for example, in order to remain financially stable.

First-party cookies, contextual advertising and other methods remain key, but we will discuss what this all means for Web3 later in the book.

Revenue model

Web1 was largely about building information and selling products. Web2, if we could define the common business model, has largely been based on driving user numbers to be able to generate income from advertising. For example, Spotify is a freemium model, which means that it offers users a limited free access level, therefore attracting over 500 million users (Demandsage, 2023), which it can then tempt, tease and upsell to a paid model.

Social media networks such as Facebook and X (formerly Twitter) have focused entirely on building products that are completely free to the user and then monetizing that data through advertising. This has changed recently on X where Elon Musk has introduced other income streams such as paid verified status.

Other more traditional subscription models have been successful too of course, such as Netflix and Amazon Prime, where unique, exclusive assets can only be accessed through a monthly payment.

If we consider the points tackled above, it becomes clear that simply attracting larger numbers of users in order to monetize their data will become increasingly challenging. This is not to say that an advertising-based or freemium model does not work, but that these models need to offer experiences where users will be willing to spend time, engage deeply and provide insights about themselves freely in exchange for value.

Paid services will remain, of course, and you can expect advertising to remain, but if we as marketers can ensure that our products deliver fast, positive experiences and outcomes for our consumers, then we can continue to deliver brand awareness and sales through revenue models that work for everyone. More on this later in the book.

The human web

One thing that has become quite clear during Web2 (but I think we already knew) is that we as humans love community. We are at our best when we're together – we are stronger, smarter and happier – and thousands of studies have confirmed this. Humans have thrived for millennia because we've lived in communities and Web2 has allowed us to engage and interact in ways that simply weren't possible in the early web. This is a great thing and the early days of social media reconnected lost friends, brought new lovers together and enabled families to share and store precious moments.

Sadly, we have to say that online communities have also had their negatives. As every city has its 'wrong side of the tracks', many online communities have had issues. From personal information being hacked (as we've already discussed in this chapter) to internet trolls and broader mental health concerns, these communities have delivered some challenges that we need to overcome in Web3.

What started as sharing precious moments developed into an unspoken competition of who could share the most impressive moments. This created some beautiful photos and stories but also led to some serious FOMO (fear of missing out). Some of these photos shared across social media today are heavily edited or even completely faked. Some show lifestyles that most of us simply can never attain and others show us something upsetting, such as an ex-partner in a new relationship or even just a friend on holiday when you really need a break.

Alongside that issue is the more obviously negative issue of internet trolls and cyber bullying. It is easier than ever to bully someone, to complain to a company or to have an argument as anyone can now do it from almost any location at any time and often with complete anonymity. This means being able to let out one's worst thoughts and feelings with no fear of reprisal or even identification. That power can enable bullies to create serious fear in young people and adults, but more than that, it can bring out the worst in people who otherwise might not stoop to such behaviours. In Web3 we need to find a way to tackle this – we'll look at this later in the book.

We also need to consider how we handle user-generated content in Web2. In Web2 there has been a huge rise in communities that have given advice and helped to solve problems. Sites such as Reddit, Quora and even YouTube exist due to UGC and of course it is the fun fundamental essence of social media. However, UGC enables individuals to mislead others, to create fake reviews (good or bad) and even to insert malware links into websites. This absolutely must be tackled and moderated more effectively in Web3.

Finally, we should briefly discuss what I call digital health. This includes some of the mental health considerations I mention above but it also includes a need to manage how we interact with technology. FOMO has not just created the issues mentioned above, it has also created a notification culture. One where we cannot switch off. Where many of us spend the majority of our downtime looking at devices and checking messages. Where the first thing we do in the morning and the last thing we do at night is check our phone. This kind of obsession with staying in touch with updates is not what humans are built for. It will create problems with our physical and mental health and I believe issues such as vision, RSI and stress-induced illness will have a significant impact on society by the mid-21st century if we do not take action on this now.

The power of the consumer

As social media has grown, the ability for a consumer to shout very loudly about an issue with a brand has created many situations where brands have had to publicly apologize or offer large-scale compensation for specific issues. Issues for which those brands may have offered only minor compensation or ignored completely before social media.

CASE STUDY

British Airways

There are many examples of potentially poor customer service on social media and this one is worth highlighting, not because it is an extreme example but quite the opposite. This is a mistake that can easily happen in many companies' social media and customer service processes, but it can quickly escalate. Also, large companies should do better.

British Airways lost a passenger's luggage. Airlines lose passengers' luggage fairly frequently and so this is clearly not the extent of the issue. What happened next was that the passenger's son, Hassan Syed, paid to promote a tweet complaining about British Airways' customer service. This was quite an extreme response, of course, but he did take the time to tag BA in the tweet, which read: 'Don't fly @BritishAirways. Their customer service is horrendous.'

The tweet received 25,000 impressions in its first six hours alone and was seen by over 70,000 users.

The real issue was that, despite being tagged, British Airways didn't respond to the promoted tweet for eight hours. This meant it had plenty of time to reach a large audience without a response – making it more impactful every minute.

I should add that BA did eventually respond and released a statement about the luggage being returned, so this is not a reflection of their performance with the lost luggage situation. The issue is that a company that operates a global airline 24/7 did not actively monitor its Twitter account 24/7 and respond quickly enough to stop this from becoming a brand-impacting issue (WeAnswer, 2024).

The British Airways case study illustrates what one person can do in just a few seconds today. This means that, as we enter Web3, brands need to consider their communications strategy, their customer service principles and more to create an always-on mentality. This could be human or AI-powered of course, but consumers expect more than ever and have more power than ever to let you know when you fall below these expectations.

SEO is dead

OK, we've been saying this for 20 years now but this time… it's still not dead.

SEO is of course going to go through a radical change as we build Web3, but SEO in 2024 is radically different to SEO in 1999. It is bigger and stronger than ever and the core principles that make up modern SEO are the same that underlined it in 1999 and should remain largely the same through to 2040 and beyond.

There are still people who try to cheat the system and get around the ethics of SEO. Those that, as in any science, will try to beat the game. There is something to be said for the effort and intelligence of those that manage to manipulate the search engines, but while those qualities can be admired, the approach should not be. Black hat SEO is likely to remain as long as there is an algorithm or AI to try to beat, but I hope we can increasingly move away from it over the coming years.

As AI takes hold and search behaviours change, SEO will become much more about answering questions and taking people directly to relevant destinations rather than the (dare I say it) outdated approach of listing paragraphs of text for people to scroll through. We'll discuss the changing face of search in Section Two of this book.

We've seen cross-device SEO, we've seen structured data playing an important role, we've seen the importance of content marketing grow enormously and we've seen punishments for those delivering poor experiences or attempting to manipulate results. I don't see any of those going away, and in fact, as AI takes hold and we get straight to the answers and experiences we want, much of this will be automated. What we should expect is marketers delivering unique value through expertise and experiences that pull a consumer to their platforms and environments.

Algorithm updates remain a key focus for SEOs and headlines are made with each major change, but I expect that to change as a more open relationship is built within the environments that users step into. Search is unlikely to disappear, but it may take another form and that is one that consumers, marketers and tech firms will need to cooperate on.

Omnichannel

As we have touched on a few times already, omnichannel marketing has been here for many years and is here to stay. We do not operate in a bubble. No consumer uses one device, one browser and one channel to conduct all their activities.

Even with the onset of the metaverse, which has the potential to enable users to complete most of their activities in one place, we cannot expect consumers to be fully immersed in that environment at all times.

Great omnichannel experiences, in fact, include the movement of users to the places where they are most comfortable. Whether that is app, email, in-store, website or anywhere else, we should be enabling users to do what is easiest and more convenient for them.

CASE STUDY
Disney World

Disney has a great integrated, omnichannel experience built around its Disney World experience.

It starts with a beautifully designed and well-built website that is fully mobile responsive and immersive. From here users can plan their experience, research everything and get a true feeling for what the fun and the logistics will be like.

Once customers have booked their trip, they can use the My Disney Experience tool to plan every little detail from the rides, dining, entertainment and more – giving the customers not just a clear plan but a reason to get excited. This becomes an experience, not just a vacation.

Once customers arrive at Disney World, they can use the dedicated mobile app to find attractions, see wait times and get the most out of the day. And it doesn't stop there – customers can then join the Magic Band program, a device that stores photos of you with the Disney characters, orders food and even becomes your hotel door key.

This approach uses multiple platforms and devices to offer an end-to-end experience to users which turns a busy, hectic day into a smooth, easy experience. A great example of omnichannel.

Control

Major players in Web2 have been controlling their fields. By that I mean that Google has largely dictated the direction search has headed, Meta has built or bought major platforms to control social media, messaging and social advertising, Amazon has controlled online retail and played quite a role in the direction of offline retail as well. This has been impressive, of course, and marketers have been able to tap into these platforms to access advertising and content opportunities among much more, as we have already mentioned.

However, monopoly regulators exist for a reason. The power of these huge businesses (and their wealthy owners) creates scenarios where people and circumstances can be manipulated for the gains of those organizations. Some large businesses in this position have been able to avoid tax, in turn impacting the economy of countries (or perhaps failing to impact the economy as they should). They have been able to circumnavigate regulations and avoid political outcomes which organizations with less power would not be able to.

As we move into Web3, decentralization comes into focus. Enabling the technology and underlying infrastructure of what happens online to take place through many thousands of touch points removes the need for these large organizations and reduces their power. This in turn puts the power back with the consumer and contributes to solving many of the issues above. This will of course come with its own issues and we will look at those later in the book. Blockchain is perhaps the most obvious place to consider this in detail and so we'll discuss this when we reach that chapter.

Free speech

I don't intend to get bogged down in politics here. Who has free speech, who thinks they have free speech and what really is free speech anyway are not questions I'm going to try to answer here. Instead, I want to pose a challenge to marketers: to think about what this really means and how this plays out in the consumers' space. We are all influenced by those around us and we see what algorithms and targeted messaging want us to see. We live in an echo chamber, surrounded by those with similar views. This is not unique to the digital age: humans have always flocked to those with similar opinions as it is comforting and safe.

What we as marketers need to consider is what this means for our messaging. Web2 has seen countless examples of this. For example, we have mentioned both the election of Donald Trump and the Brexit referendum in this chapter. Both of those are well known for having two firmly opposed sides and both sides were certain they were going to win up until the result was revealed. Why? Because everyone they were surrounded by, both on and offline, was agreeing with them. This is due to their friend circle and perhaps some manipulation (as mentioned above).

As we move into Web3 it's important for marketers to be responsible in their thinking and also to consider what their targeted audience may be exposed to. If they are in a segment, cohort or demographic that is likely to be surrounded by specific messaging, how will they react to your campaign and how can you personalize the message to ensure it works for each individual?

Beyond this, the other core element to consider is where to draw the line on free speech. This is a difficult point to come to wide-scale agreement on, but there is a line to draw, especially on social media, between allowing anyone to say anything to anyone and ensuring that hate speech, misinformation and bullying are not allowed. The social networks have a responsibility to moderate and ensure inappropriate messages are not seen by users, especially children. But also consumers and marketers have a responsibility to call this behaviour out and demand action. This is a key point to focus on over the coming years.

Conclusion

Web2 has brought us some phenomenal experiences but also many challenges. We have an opportunity now, as we step into Web3, to create new experiences and approaches to data, targeting, personalization, messaging, ethics and much more. We can reinvent and position ourselves for the future by taking a stance and engaging with our audiences on the journey. We'll dig into all of this and what it means over the coming chapters.

Notes

Brown, A J (2020) 'Should I stay or should I leave?': Exploring (dis)continued Facebook Use after the Cambridge Analytica scandal. Social Media + Society, 6(1). https://doi.org/10.1177/2056305120913884 (archived at https://perma.cc/G3K2-N5JC)

Demandsage (2023) Spotify stats for 2024 (users, artists, & revenue). 15 February, www.demandsage.com/spotify-stats/#:~:text=It%20is%20estimated%20that%20 Spotify,and%20creators%20on%20its%20platform.&text=Spotify%20has%20 551%20million%20monthly,of%20Spotify's%20monthly%20active%20listeners (archived at https://perma.cc/4M26-GW3Y)

Gartner (2021) Gartner predicts the opt-out rate for mobile app tracking will decline from 85% to 60% by 2023. 2 December, www.gartner.com/en/newsroom/press-releases/2021-12-02-gartner-predicts-the-opt-out-rate-for-mobile-app-trac#:~:text=of%20Digital%20Experience-,The%20opt%2Dout%20rate%20 for%20mobile%20app%20tracking%20will%20decline,%2C%20according%20 20to%20Gartner%2C%20Inc (archived at https://perma.cc/7Q5Y-B5CM)

Google (2021) Charting a course towards a more privacy-first web. 3 March, https://blog.google/products/ads-commerce/a-more-privacy-first-web/ (archived at https://perma.cc/9SE4-ZJFW)

Hubspot (2022) The death of the third-party cookie: What marketers need to know about Google's 2023 phase-out. 27 July, https://blog.hubspot.com/marketing/third-party-cookie-phase-out (archived at https://perma.cc/GYE6-6R29)

Statcounter (2024) Chrome browser market share. https://gs.statcounter.com/browser-market-share/desktop/worldwide/#monthly-200901-202401 (archived at https://perma.cc/9RVK-CXZX)

Statista (2023) Annual number of data compromises and individuals impacted in the United States from 2005 to 2023. 12 February, www.statista.com/statistics/273550/data-breaches-recorded-in-the-united-states-by-number-of-breaches-and-records-exposed/ (archived at https://perma.cc/6DU9-4GZL)

Statista (2024) Share of adults who understood vs. did not understand how internet cookies worked in the United States as of October 2022. 10 January, www.statista.com/statistics/1342040/understand-cookies-usa/ (archived at https://perma.cc/MJ9T-N6BA)

WeAnswer (2024) BA case study. https://web.archive.org/web/20231208024548/ www.weanswer.co.uk/insights/british-airways-social-customer-service-debacle (archived at https://perma.cc/QQ2H-Q668)

3

Understanding the Semantic Web

Semantic technologies play a vital role in Web 3.0 and have the potential to transform how information is accessed by humans and understood by machines. In this chapter I'll talk about technologies including semantic search and how marketers are starting to adapt and leverage the new opportunities that are arising.

A QUICK NOTE ON THE TERM 'SEMANTIC'

The term 'semantic' relates to the meaning of words, phrases, symbols or other elements of language. It deals with the study of meaning and how words or symbols convey information, concepts or ideas. In a broader sense, 'semantic' can refer to anything related to the interpretation, understanding and representation of meaning, not just in language but also in various contexts such as logic, computer science and information retrieval. In the context of the Semantic Web and semantic search, it pertains to understanding and representing the meaning of data and information to improve communication and data processing. It also refers to the combination of multiple sources of information to create contextually accurate results and answers to queries.

What is the Semantic Web?

The Semantic Web is an evolution of the World Wide Web in which content will be more understandable by computers. It involves using standardized formats and protocols to add meaning to web content, enabling better data integration and interpretation. Ultimately, the goal is to create a web where information can be easily linked, interpreted and processed by machines, leading to more intelligent and automated applications. In turn, users will have a more streamlined experience in which information is easier to find.

Tim Berners-Lee actually envisioned the Semantic Web back in 1999. He spoke about a decentralized internet and used a helpful analogy to visualize it. He said that if you think of the web as putting all the documents in the world into one big book, then consider the Semantic Web as turning all those documents into one big database or mathematical formula. Effectively this creates a scientific indexing of the web (W3, 2024).

Progress was made over the years that followed, but the sweeping changes and broad adoption that many had hoped for have not fully materialized. The World Wide Web Consortium (W3C) had been actively developing standards for the Semantic Web, including the Resource Description Framework (RDF). Essentially, the RDF was a simple way of conveying the meaning of information in sets of three properties. There was also Web Ontology Language (OWL) and SPARQL. Like RDF, OWL was another framework for processing and integrating data on the web and has now developed into a family of different languages with different syntaxes and specifications. SPARQL however is a query language for databases able to retrieve and manipulate data stored in RDF format.

The concept of the Semantic Web is such an important foundation of Web 3.0 that the terms are sometimes used interchangeably. This highlights the significance of semantics in the bigger picture of where the internet is heading and the key tenets of decentralization, interconnected data and making that data readable by machines.

The Semantic Web and the metaverse

The Semantic Web has significant implications for the development and evolution of the metaverse. The metaverse is often visualized as a collective virtual shared space, a convergence of virtually augmented physical reality, augmented virtuality and the persistent virtual space. However, the metaverse will not be just one shared virtual space; it will consist of multiple virtual worlds, platforms and environments. As such, there's a need for interoperability – the ability for diverse systems and organizations to work together seamlessly. The Semantic Web can provide the structured data framework required to ensure that different metaverse platforms can communicate, understand and interact with each other's data.

As mentioned in Chapter 2, omnichannel is going to be just as important in terms of the metaverse as it is in any other context. The Semantic Web will enhance our ability to provide omnichannel experiences for complex interactions between metaverse and non-metaverse channels.

To sum up, the Semantic Web can act as the underlying framework that makes the metaverse not just a collection of virtual spaces but a coherent, interconnected, intelligent and user-centric environment.

A note on structured data

Structured data has been around for a long time and is a fundamental element of the Semantic Web. Essentially, the term 'structured data' refers to sets of data that are labelled in a way that makes the data machine readable. One of the early attempts to add meaning to data was the Meta Content Framework (nothing to do with Facebook). This model took inspiration from an area in computer science called knowledge representation and connects data in a web-like form known as a directed labelled graph. The intention was to develop a single graph to represent a wide range of data entities from different websites, as this would enable different applications to work with data from different sites. It is said that Berners-Lee was very optimistic about this approach. Many standards for tagging data were developed in the years to follow, such as RDF and OWL (ACM Queue, 2015).

Different types of markup with different syntax had been in use since the early days, which of course was not ideal in terms of interoperability. So, in 2011, Schema.org was created in order to provide a single form of markup for all content – now known as schema markup. By using the correct tags to structure data for online properties, you are enabling algorithms and search engines to understand that data and how to connect it. So, marketers now use schema markup to provide search engines with richer information about their content, leading to more precise search results and better SEO rankings.

The same applies with voice search. As it becomes more prevalent, marketers will need to optimize their content to match natural language queries, taking into account context and user intent for voice search optimization. Semantic web technologies also support local SEO efforts by helping search engines understand location-based queries, which marketers use for geotargeted advertising and personalized content delivery based on a user's location.

The need for structured data may actually diminish as natural language processing (NLP) and AI technologies continue to improve in understanding and processing unstructured data (more about those technologies later).

Semantic search

Semantic search aims to enhance the accuracy and relevance of search results, making it easier for users to find the information they're looking for, especially when dealing with ambiguous or complex queries. In 2013, Google released a major update to its algorithm, known as Hummingbird. The intention was that this update would drastically improve the understanding of search intent and take the Semantic Web from theory to practice.

Instead of relying on keywords like traditional search algorithms do, semantic search is all about understanding the context and meaning behind the words used in a query. The result is that more relevant search results are delivered by considering the intent and context of the user's query rather than just matching keywords.

Semantic search uses NLP and machine learning algorithms to analyse the relationships between words, phrases and concepts in documents and queries. Search engines can then discern the user's intent behind a query, even if the query doesn't match the words in the documents being searched. But how can the algorithms understand context and search intent? There are a number of ways.

One primary approach is by using NLP (see below) to analyse the context in which words are used, delving deeper into the surrounding terms and their relationships. Personalization further aids in deciphering search intent; by incorporating a user's search history and their preferences, search engines can tailor results more aptly. Another technique is query expansion, where the algorithm broadens queries to encompass synonyms, related terms and concepts. Lastly, entity recognition allows them to pinpoint and comprehend specific entities, be they people, places or things, within documents and queries, thereby delivering more accurate search outcomes.

What is NLP?

Natural language processing is a branch of artificial intelligence that focuses on the interaction between computers and human language. It encompasses the development of algorithms and models that enable computers to understand, interpret and generate human language in a way that is both meaningful and useful.

NLP forms the basis of a wide range of tasks and applications. For example, it enables computers to understand the meaning of written text through tasks like sentiment analysis, where the model can determine the sentiment (positive, negative, neutral) expressed in a piece of text (useful for social media monitoring and customer feedback analysis). In fact, it's already used for information retrieval in search engines, even though the search experience is not yet fully semantic.

Text-generation uses of NLP include question answering such as chatbot responses, autocomplete suggestions and even content generation (we're all aware of how ChatGPT is disrupting many industries).

Another key area to watch out for is speech recognition. NLP techniques convert spoken language into written text, which is the basis for voice assistants like Siri or speech-to-text systems. In fact, the number of voice assistants in use in 2020 was 4.2 billion worldwide and this figure was projected to reach 8.4 billion in 2024

(Statista, 2022). In addition, one in four adults in the US already have a smart speaker device in their homes and the global smart speaker market was projected to exceed $30 billion by 2024 (Sterling, 2020; GMI, 2018). Users are already conducting around 1 billion voice searches per month, so this is going to be a vital aspect of Web 3.0 (Shewale, 2024).

When users speak their query into Google, they often use full sentences that would be spoken in casual conversation, such as 'What were the best films released in 2023?'. This is in contrast to a traditional search query, which may look something like 'best films 2023'. As a result, algorithms are adapting in order to process these natural language queries effectively.

NLP relies on techniques like machine learning, deep learning and linguistic analysis to process and understand language. It's a rapidly evolving field with applications in various industries, including healthcare, finance, customer service and more, where natural language understanding and generation are essential for improving communication and decision-making processes.

More applications of semantic technologies in marketing

Aside from content optimization and semantic search, how else is semantics already being used? Marketers integrate chatbots and virtual assistants into websites and applications, leveraging semantic understanding to provide more meaningful and context-aware responses to user inquiries, enhancing customer support and engagement. Semantic technologies also aid in the creation and curation of content. Marketers can use language models such as GPT-4 to generate articles, product descriptions and social media posts, saving time and resources.

The metaverse will likely see an increase in AI-powered agents and bots, assisting users with various tasks. The Semantic Web can enhance the capabilities of these agents, allowing them to better understand user requests, retrieve relevant information and even perform complex tasks based on the semantic understanding of the environment.

Semantic technologies are also the key to more effective personalization. Again, analysing user data and preferences allows for personalized content recommendations, which enhances user engagement and drives conversions by delivering content relevant to individual interests. Email campaigns benefit from better open rates and click-through rates, while advertising campaigns can target users based on the content they consume, their interests and their online behaviour.

Naturally, the Semantic Web has important implications in advertising. Advanced semantic algorithms analyse the content on web pages that users visit in order to understand the context and overarching theme of the content, which can then be used to display more relevant contextual ads to users. In addition, a user's browsing history and behavioural data can inform targeting, providing a detailed profile of the user's interests, preferences and potential needs.

The Semantic Web also has the potential to make data analysis far more robust than it is now. Structured frameworks enable the integration of diverse data sources by mapping how data from one source relates to data from another. As such, integrating data from various channels like social media, websites and customer relationship management (CRM) systems gives marketers a comprehensive view of a customer's journey, which is vital for understanding touchpoints, behaviour patterns and preferences, and makes all the difference when developing omnichannel strategies.

The last area I'll talk about is link building. Tools that use semantic web technologies can scan the web to find content that is contextually similar or related to a marketer's content. Again, this goes beyond just finding keyword overlaps; the tools understand the essence and context of content, finding opportunities for marketers to add value to their respective audiences by linking their content. Another benefit of this approach is that while traditional backlink tools might identify sites that could be linked based on keywords, semantic technologies can find sites that might be contextually relevant even if they don't use the exact keywords. This can uncover more strategic opportunities for building high-quality backlinks that otherwise might be missed.

The Semantic Web and IoT

The Semantic Web can add more value to IoT applications by adding a layer of semantic meaning to the data generated and exchanged by IoT devices. Adding meaning to IoT data enables more efficient data integration, interoperability and meaningful analysis. Consider applications such as smart homes and industrial automation – semantic data can be used to make more informed decisions and automate processes intelligently.

Another important consideration is variation among data formats. As mentioned, standards like RDF and OWL allow data to be standardized so that IoT devices can communicate and understand each other's data, even if they use different vocabularies or data structures. This interoperability is crucial for creating IoT ecosystems where devices from different manufacturers can work together seamlessly.

Naturally, analytics is the next step in many scenarios where IoT technology is implemented. Again, semantic standards support complex queries that go beyond simple keyword-based searches, allowing users to ask questions about IoT data in a more natural and meaningful way. IoT data can also be integrated into knowledge graphs, which are interconnected networks of data that represent real-world relationships. This enables more comprehensive and insightful analysis.

Overall, the Semantic Web can enhance the capabilities of IoT by providing a framework for standardized, interoperable and semantically rich data. This in turn enables more advanced and context-aware applications and services in today's connected home.

Semantic Web case studies

Case studies on Semantic Web technologies are emerging in a huge range of contexts, from law to healthcare to automotive diagnostics. It's definitely worth looking into what's happening in different sectors for inspiration on how these use cases could translate across industries. But for our purposes, let's consider some examples of how the Semantic Web is being leveraged for marketing.

CASE STUDY

Volkswagen's contextual search project

German automobile manufacturer Volkswagen ventured into the realm of semantic technology back in 2010 when the company decided to implement contextual search on its website. The primary goal was to enhance site search, allowing users to access relevant information quickly, thus facilitating faster decision-making and enhancing conversion rates. It also aimed to display related content, even if the user was not directly looking for it, offering a chance to highlight strategically important information.

I won't go into the technical stuff, but in essence the company used a range of established vocabularies for labelling data, including GoodRelations (a type of web ontology language) and some industry-specific vocabularies. The revamped search system could understand context so that users could search using detailed parameters, such as 'cars priced between x and y with engine power greater than z, available in red, and having user reviews of more than four stars'. This level of granularity in search was previously unattainable and delivered a comprehensive solution for users.

Operationally, Volkswagen reaped numerous benefits, such as smoother collaborations with third parties. One notable collaboration was with the used car locator application, which was integrated seamlessly using the same semantic principles. An added advantage was the enhancement of content visibility to major search engines, fostering a more comprehensive digital presence (Greenly et al., 2011).

CASE STUDY

The Financial Times: Semantic advertising

Online publishers can use semantic technologies to get higher click-through rates and prevent ad misplacement (such as displaying ads for Greek holidays next to articles on riots in Athens, as once happened on the website of *The Guardian* newspaper in the UK).

Back in 2011, the *Financial Times* started trialling SmartMatch, a tool from Smartology to which brands could opt in. The tool would analyse content in real-time and ensure that only relevant and appropriate ads were placed on the page. Brands that used the tool are said to have seen a tenfold increase in ad engagement rates. As such, many brands now use such tools (O'Reilly, 2013).

Conclusion

The concept of the Semantic Web has been around for decades and Berners-Lee was very optimistic about its development in the late 1990s and early 2000s. While the web is not yet fully semantic, we are getting there and the various applications of this technology are steadily growing in prevalence. Marketers need to be familiar with these applications and leverage them for a better user experience and more effective campaigns.

Notes

ACM Queue (2015) Schema.org: Evolution of structured data on the web. 15 December, https://queue.acm.org/detail.cfm?id=2857276 (archived at https://perma.cc/MN6L-TJJA)

GMI (2018) Smart speaker market size by intelligent virtual assistant (Alexa, Google Assistant, Siri, Cortana, Others), by application (personal, professional, commercial), industry analysis report, regional outlook, growth potential, competitive market share & forecast, 2018–2024. www.gminsights.com/industry-analysis/smart-speaker-market (archived at https://perma.cc/PCY6-WQTB)

Greenly, W, Sanderman-Craik, C, Otero, Y and Streit, J (2011) Case study: Contextual search for Volkswagen and the automotive industry, W3. October, www.w3.org/2001/sw/sweo/public/UseCases/Volkswagen/ (archived at https://perma.cc/39KN-PS3T)

O'Reilly, L (2013) FT.com opens up 'semantic advertising' to prevent ad misplacement. Marketing Week, 11 December, www.marketingweek.com/ft-com-opens-up-semantic-advertising-to-prevent-ad-misplacement/ (archived at https://perma.cc/CG67-EV7S)

Shewale, R (2024) 67 voice search statistics for 2024, (updated data). 11 January, www.demandsage.com/voice-search-statistics/ (archived at https://perma.cc/B94Z-Z4XH)

Statista (2022) Number of digital voice assistants in use worldwide from 2019 to 2024 (in billions). 14 March, www.statista.com/statistics/973815/worldwide-digital-voice-assistant-in-use/ (archived at https://perma.cc/EUE3-CJ45)

Sterling, G (2020) Roughly 1 in 4 U.S. adults now owns a smart speaker, according to new report. 9 January, https://martech.org/roughly-1-in-4-u-s-adults-now-owns-a-smart-speaker-according-to-new-report/ (archived at https://perma.cc/HX3H-MP8G)

W3 (2024) The Semantic Web. www.w3.org/2000/Talks/0906-xmlweb-tbl/text.htm#:~:text=Like%20good%20government%2C%20it%20must,or%20one%20big%20mathematical%20formula (archived at https://perma.cc/CNR4-RXUG)

4

What blockchain means for marketing

With today's focus on transparency, security and efficiency, blockchain has emerged as a revolutionary force poised to reshape numerous industries. In this chapter we'll examine the transformative potential of blockchain within marketing and Web3 as a whole.

What is blockchain?

The origin of blockchain technology is closely tied to the creation of Bitcoin. In 2008, an individual or group using the pseudonym Satoshi Nakamoto published a whitepaper titled 'Bitcoin: A peer-to-peer electronic cash system'. This paper introduced the concept of a decentralized digital currency system that operated without the need for a central authority or intermediaries and it described the underlying technology – blockchain – that made this possible.

At its core, a blockchain is a decentralized ledger of all transactions across a network. Think of it like a public record book – instead of a single person or organization managing it, it's distributed across many computers connected over the internet. With blockchain, information is grouped into 'blocks', like pages in a ledger, and these blocks are linked together in a 'chain' in chronological order. When one block is full, a new one is created and it links to the previous one.

Once data is recorded on the blockchain, it cannot be changed, which provides transparency and security. This decentralized model also makes it possible for participants to confirm transactions without the need for a central clearing authority. Every entity (also known as a 'node') on the network checks and verifies transactions, making it highly secure and while anyone can see the entire ledger, they can't see who the transactions belong to.

While Bitcoin was the first application of blockchain technology, the potential of blockchain extends far beyond cryptocurrencies. Its decentralized, tamper-proof nature has made it an attractive option for a multitude of use cases in numerous industries.

Blockchain, cryptocurrency and the future of digital currency

Cryptocurrency: here to stay or just a fad?

The future of cryptocurrency is a subject of ongoing debate, but there are several factors suggesting that it's likely here to stay in some form. First of all, cryptocurrencies like Bitcoin and Ethereum have gained significant popularity and adoption since their inception and they are now accepted by a growing number of businesses for payments and investments. In addition, large financial institutions are showing increasing interest in cryptocurrencies and some are investing in or offering cryptocurrency-related products and services, adding credibility to the space. These digital currencies have also sparked innovations such as decentralized finance (DeFi) platforms, which offer alternatives to traditional financial services.

Governments and regulatory bodies are working on establishing clearer frameworks for cryptocurrency regulation, which is likely to help legitimize the industry and reduce uncertainty. However, challenges remain, including price volatility, scalability issues and environmental concerns related to energy consumption.

Again, blockchain technology has proven to have valuable applications beyond cryptocurrency, so the underlying technology is likely to persist and evolve, continuing to shape the future in disruptive ways.

CASE STUDY

Burger King's 'Whoppercoin' campaign

How are brands applying cryptocurrency in their marketing campaigns? One notable case study is Burger King Russia's 'Whoppercoin' campaign. In August 2017, the fast-food giant launched its own cryptocurrency called 'Whoppercoin' as part of a loyalty programme. Customers received one Whoppercoin for each ruble they spent on a Whopper burger; they could then collect and trade these coins.

The programme was built on the Ethereum blockchain, making it a genuine cryptocurrency with a decentralized ledger. Customers simply needed to download a special app to manage their Whoppercoins and this app acted as a digital wallet for the currency. That's right – the campaign was not just about collecting points that could be exchanged for the company's own products, as is the case in many reward programmes. These coins were tradable on crypto exchanges, allowing customers to convert them to fiat currency or other cryptocurrencies. This made the programme unique and the novel use of cryptocurrency generated hype, while customers felt that they were getting something back from the company.

Through this campaign, Burger King Russia garnered international media attention, enhancing its visibility and reinforcing its image as an innovative brand. While it was primarily a marketing stunt rather than a long-term cryptocurrency initiative, it demonstrated how using gamification – combined with a novel technology – could get customers excited about the brand, generate repeat business and increase brand awareness (Martineau, 2017).

Cryptocurrency scandals

While cryptocurrency has many benefits, it's seen its share of scandals and controversies over the years, a classic example being the case of Mt Gox. Mt Gox was one of the earliest and largest cryptocurrency exchanges and in 2014 it filed for bankruptcy after losing 850,000 bitcoins (worth approximately $450 million at the time) due to hacking and mismanagement.

Another case involving lost currency was that of Canadian crypto exchange QuadrigaCX. The exchange faced controversy when its founder, Gerald Cotten, died unexpectedly in 2018. He was the only one with access to the exchange's private keys and millions of dollars in cryptocurrency became inaccessible, leading to bankruptcy proceedings.

Of course, not all cases of lost currency are the result of error. A more sinister scenario known as the 'exit scam' occurs when cryptocurrency projects and exchanges abruptly shut down and disappear with users' funds. The most famous case was the Bitpetite scam, where the founders vanished after collecting investments.

The dawn of cryptocurrencies also unlocked new opportunities for fraudsters to launch Ponzi schemes, such as Bitconnect. Bitconnect was a lending and exchange platform that promised high returns on investments in its own cryptocurrency, Bitconnect Coin (BCC). It turned out to be a Ponzi scheme and the value of BCC collapsed, resulting in substantial financial losses for many investors. A similar case was PlusToken, a large-scale Ponzi scheme that defrauded investors of billions of dollars. It also played a significant role in the manipulation of crypto markets.

OneCoin was yet another fraudulent pyramid scheme. The coin was promoted as a cryptocurrency and billions of dollars were raised from investors worldwide, but there was no real blockchain or cryptocurrency behind it. Its founders faced legal action in multiple countries. Numerous initial coin offerings (ICOs) also turned out to be scams; projects promised innovative blockchain solutions but never delivered, resulting in the loss of investors' funds. Prominent examples included Centra Tech and Pincoin/iFan.

Pump-and-dump schemes (typically associated with low-cap currencies) also happen in the crypto world. Groups artificially inflate the price of a currency through coordinated buying (pumping) and then sell off (dumping) to unsuspecting investors.

These examples highlight the risks associated with the cryptocurrency space, making it crucial for investors to exercise caution, conduct thorough research and use reputable platforms to minimize these risks. Additionally, regulatory authorities have been taking steps to address fraudulent activities in the industry.

Price volatility

Bitcoin, like other cryptocurrencies, has experienced significant price volatility throughout its history. During its early spike in 2011, its price surged from less than $1 to over $31 before crashing back down to a few dollars; this early volatility was driven by limited liquidity and speculative trading. Towards the end of 2013, Bitcoin reached around $1,000 on Mt Gox but when the exchange filed for bankruptcy several months later, its price dropped dramatically, falling to around $200.

The coin's value began to rise again in 2017, reaching nearly $20,000 in December of that year. This was driven by increased mainstream interest, media coverage and speculation, but the price then corrected and dropped below $3,000 in 2018. Another significant price increase occurred from late 2020 into early 2021, reaching an all-time high of over $60,000 in April 2021. This rally was fuelled by institutional investment and growing acceptance of Bitcoin as a store of value. However, in mid-2021, China intensified its crackdown on cryptocurrency activities, leading to a sharp drop in Bitcoin's price; it went from around $60,000 to under $30,000 in a matter of weeks (Partz, 2022).

FIGURE 4.1 Bitcoin price in US dollars 2010–2024

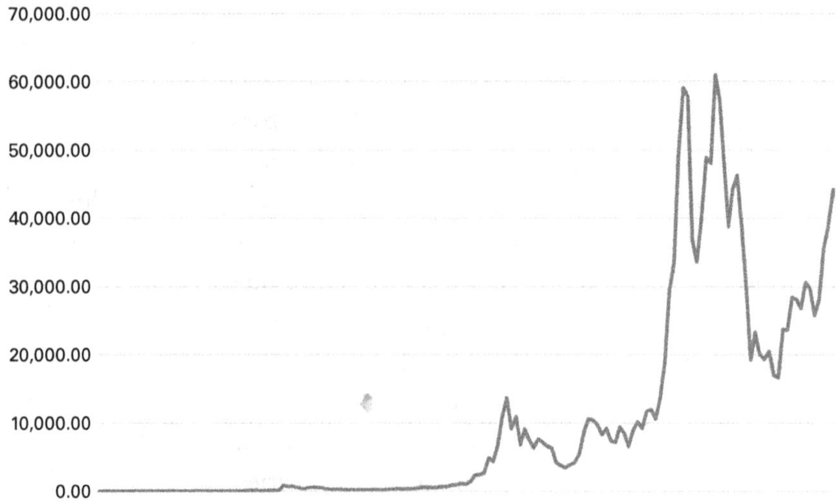

SOURCE Adapted from Webster, 2024

Bitcoin: the outlook

When considering the outlook for Bitcoin over the next 10 years, it's important to note that cryptocurrency markets are highly speculative and influenced by a wide range of variables, making it challenging to predict long-term price movements. With that said, there are a few important factors that give us some clues about its trajectory.

As I mentioned, institutional interest and investment in Bitcoin continue to grow. More companies and financial institutions are offering Bitcoin-related services, which could contribute to increased stability. Its stability may also improve as the market matures, the coin becoming less prone to extreme price swings, akin to how traditional financial markets operate. Bitcoin's fixed supply (21 million coins) and its 'halving' events, which reduce the rate of new coin creation, could continue to drive demand and potentially increase its value. Regulatory developments will also play a crucial role in Bitcoin's future; clear and favourable regulations could encourage broader adoption, while adverse regulations could hinder growth.

It's also important to consider that cryptocurrency mining is an energy-intensive endeavour. The annual energy use associated with Bitcoin alone is 127.46 TWh, which is comparable to the consumption of the United Arab Emirates. However, not all coins are equal; some of the algorithms involved in cryptocurrency mining are more energy demanding than others. In 2022, the algorithm used in the Ethereum network was changed from the so-called 'proof-of-work' to 'proof-of-stake', reducing its energy consumption by 99.84 per cent. If other currencies make such changes, there may be less chance of regulators stepping in (Digiconomist, 2023).

The role of cryptocurrency in the development of Web3

The decentralized nature of cryptocurrency makes it the perfect catalyst for creating a decentralized internet. As such, it has laid the foundation for many new types of services that we will use in the future. One example is decentralized apps, or dApps. Unlike traditional apps that reside on central servers like AWS, dApps aren't confined to a single point of control; instead, they are distributed across various nodes. Take an app under Meta's umbrella, for example. Right now, user data is stored on their servers, but in future it may be dispersed across numerous servers and personal devices, stored in encrypted fragments. Essentially, all data exchange is peer-to-peer with dApps.

dApps are built on blockchain platforms and often use cryptocurrencies to provide access to their features. Decentralized finance, or DeFi applications, are a type of dApp that provide financial services like lending, borrowing, trading and earning interest, all without traditional banks or intermediaries.

Many dApps rely on smart contracts to carry out their functions. These self-executing contracts automate agreements and transactions in all kinds of areas, from supply chain management to voting systems. In essence, the contracts themselves are pieces of code that execute the terms of an agreement when predefined conditions are met. No trust or uncertainty is involved in these transactions, which is what makes them so appealing. The if-then involved logic also enables smart contracts to assist with workflow automation.

Many cryptocurrencies, most notably Ethereum, were created to facilitate and host smart contracts on their blockchain. Users initiate transactions from their cryptocurrency wallet; the action is then registered on a distributed database, at which point their identity is confirmed. Next, the transaction is approved and the associated code is executed. When the transaction is complete, the blockchain is updated, creating an immutable record that is viewable by parties that have been given permission.

Smart contracts are already being used in many sectors for many different purposes. For example, in California, they are used for generating marriage licences, while Arizona uses them to create enforceable legal agreements. In the Republic of Georgia, they are being used for land title registry and similar projects are being carried out in other regions, including the United Arab Emirates.

Another emerging principle is the decentralized autonomous organization (DAO), a new type of organizational structure made possible by blockchain technology. At its core, a DAO is a set of smart contracts that codify the rules and decision-making processes of an organization, removing the need for traditional hierarchical management structures. With no central authority, decisions in a DAO are made by its members.

Not only will cryptocurrency be the fuel for many Web3 applications, it will also act as the glue that holds them together; it will act as a bridge between different blockchain networks and will enable the seamless exchange of value and data across various platforms. As a result, cryptocurrency wallets will need to provide interoperability among dApps and other decentralized services.

NFTs and their potential

NFTs, or non-fungible tokens, are a type of digital asset that represent ownership or proof of authenticity of a unique item or piece of content using blockchain technology. Unlike cryptocurrencies, which are fungible and interchangeable (one Bitcoin is always equal to one Bitcoin), NFTs are unique.

Each NFT represents a specific digital item, whether it's digital art, music, videos, virtual real estate, collectibles, in-game items or any other digital content, and they provide a digital certificate of ownership. This means that the owner of an NFT can prove they own the original digital item, even though copies of that item may exist on the internet. With that said, there can be grey areas in terms of intellectual property rights of such assets; owning an NFT may grant ownership of the digital item, but it doesn't necessarily confer copyright or licensing rights to the underlying content, unless explicitly specified.

NFTs are created, bought and sold on blockchain-based platforms and can be transferred or sold across different platforms and marketplaces that support the same blockchain standards (e.g. Ethereum-based NFTs can be traded on various Ethereum-compatible platforms). The use of NFTs as a means of buying and selling digital assets has gained popularity and some have sold for significant amounts of money. Here are a few examples:

- 'The First Ever Tweet': former Twitter CEO Jack Dorsey's first tweet was sold as an NFT for $2.9 million. It represented a significant moment in the intersection of social media and NFTs.

- NBA Top Shot: this officially licensed NBA NFT platform allows fans to buy, sell and trade NBA collectible highlights. Some of these NFT 'moments' have sold for large sums.

- 'Mars House' by Krista Kim: this digital house, part of the 'Mars House' project, sold for over $500,000. It represents virtual real estate in the metaverse.

- Bored Ape Yacht Club (BAYC): this NFT project features a collection of unique hand-drawn ape characters. Owners of these NFTs gain access to exclusive events and benefits within the BAYC community.

- Axie Infinity: this blockchain-based game allows players to collect, breed and battle fantasy creatures called Axies. Some rare Axies have sold for substantial amounts.

- Beeple: pieces of digital art by artist Mike Winkelmann (a.k.a. Beeple) were sold as NFTs, including 'Everydays: The First 5000 Days', which was sold at auction for more than $69 million in 2021. This marked a major milestone for NFT art and brought widespread attention to the space. Another piece, 'Crossroads', sold for $6.6 million and gained attention for its political and social commentary.

These examples showcase the diversity of NFT use cases. Successful NFTs often have a combination of rarity, cultural significance and community engagement that drives their value, but their prices can be highly volatile and their success is subject to market dynamics and trends.

Do NFTs have a future? They gained significant attention and popularity in a relatively short period, leading some to believe they are a trend or fad driven by hype. The ecosystem is still in its early stages and there is much experimentation and innovation happening. While some early projects may not stand the test of time, the versatility of NFTs suggests they may have staying power. Reflecting on the Mars House example, it's also clear that they could have a significant role to play in the metaverse.

The impact of blockchain on marketing

We've covered a lot of detail in this chapter on cryptocurrency, NFTs and blockchain principles. These are all essential foundations in understanding how blockchain will play a role in marketing as we move into Web3. Let's now look at the impact of these initiatives and this fast-moving technology specifically in the marketing space.

Blockchain technology is changing marketing in numerous ways. First of all, creating transparent and tamper-proof records of transactions and data helps to build trust between businesses and consumers and this is particularly valuable in areas like advertising where trust issues abound. Blockchain's immutability also makes it harder for fraudsters to manipulate data, thus reducing ad fraud and ensuring that marketing metrics are accurate.

The fact that every transaction on the blockchain is anonymous means that marketers will need to incentivize customers to hand over their data. While this may seem inconvenient, in reality this is exactly what marketers should be doing today. It ensures that leads are better qualified, customers better understood and, with third-party cookies coming to an end, marketers should be building first-party data and creating communities that move them along this path already.

Another consideration about trust pertains to corporate social responsibility, something of great importance to Gen Z. Blockchain provides supply chain transparency as it enables the journey of products from source to consumer to be tracked. In turn, this allows for transparent marketing about the origin and quality of goods, which is especially important in industries such as fashion and food. There will be no room for dishonesty here and businesses that can prove their ethical practices will gain competitive advantage.

Advertising will also become decentralized. Decentralized ad networks will connect advertisers and publishers directly, reducing the need for middlemen and thereby lowering costs. These networks will give businesses more autonomy in terms of their advertising operations and consumers more control over the ads they see. In many cases, advertisers will be judged by their audience – they won't have centralized ad authorities calling the shots.

Many decentralized ad networks use their native tokens for transactions. Advertisers buy tokens to pay for ad placements and publishers or content creators receive tokens as payment for displaying ads. These tokens can then be exchanged for other cryptocurrencies or fiat money. An example of this at work is Brave Browser, which rewards users with the currency BAT each time they click on an ad. The user can also select how often they see those ads and can pause the service at any time.

As for smart contracts, they will automate various marketing activities. Here are a few examples:

- Affiliate payments: when a sale is made through an affiliate link, the contract can immediately recognize the transaction and automatically distribute commissions to the affiliate, reducing delays and disputes.

- Dynamic pricing: in sectors where prices change dynamically based on demand, inventory or other factors, smart contracts can automatically adjust pricing in real-time, ensuring optimal pricing strategies.

- Budgeting and spending: smart contracts can be programmed to release marketing budget funds only when certain conditions are met, ensuring that expenditures align with approved strategies and goals.

- Event-triggered actions: marketing campaigns often involve sequences of actions triggered by user behaviours. While marketing automation software already takes the manual work out of these processes, smart contracts may be more efficient.

There are endless ways in which smart contracts could help provide better customer experiences through partnerships. Let's consider a hypothetical partnership between a fitness app and a health food company. Every time the user achieves their weekly fitness goals, they could automatically receive a discount code for the health food company, encouraging ongoing engagement for both parties.

Conclusion

Blockchain is an integral part of the new, decentralized internet, driven by peer-to-peer networks and community interactions. Transparency, democracy and mutual benefit are key themes we can expect to see materialize in the months and years to come. Marketers today should be considering the role that cryptocurrency, smart contracts and decentralization will play in the martech space and how that relates to their specific marketing operations, goals, projects and campaigns alongside how their customers are likely to adjust to these changes. This thinking should be built into any marketing strategy that is going to be optimal and effective throughout the 2020s.

Notes

Digiconomist (2023) Bitcoin Energy Consumption Index. https://digiconomist.net/bitcoin-energyconsumption#:~:text=Bitcoin%20could%20potentially%20switch%20to,%2Dof%2Dwork%20based%20system (archived at https://perma.cc/7DQC-KRMA)

Martineau, P (2017) Burger King's Whoppercoin is the only cryptocurrency that matters. Intelligencer, NY Magazine. 24 August, https://nymag.com/intelligencer/2017/08/whoppercoin-burger-king-russias-cryptocurrency.html (archived at https://perma.cc/M4K3-VB72)

Partz, H (2022) A brief history of Bitcoin crashes and bear markets: 2009–2022. Coin Telegraph. 10 July, https://cointelegraph.com/news/a-brief-history-of-bitcoin-crashes-and-bear-markets-2009-2022 (archived at https://perma.cc/SM7Y-MKK5)

Webster, I (2024) Bitcoin historical prices. U.S. Finance Reference. www.in2013dollars.com/bitcoin-price (archived at https://perma.cc/4Z3Y-K88X)

5

Understanding the importance of gaming

Gaming principles will form a big part of Web 3.0, so it's vital to understand how gaming will feature in the new ecosystem. This chapter discusses how gaming will bring new opportunities for marketers – I'll talk about game mechanics, games within the metaverse, currency within games, decentralized gaming, how games are becoming brands and much more. Chapter 11 will be dedicated to the topic of gamification, examining game mechanics in more depth and the consumer psychology involved.

You don't need to be a gamer but you need to understand games

Even if you've never been a gamer, now is the time to learn about the principles and dynamics of gaming. Games are fuelled by interactivity, engagement and user experience – attributes we are all familiar with as marketers. As gaming mechanics such as open worlds simply the way you interact with the internet, understanding their mechanics brings valuable insights into crafting engaging, future-proof marketing strategies.

OPEN WORLDS

For those not familiar with the term, this is an important one to understand as we move into Web3. An open world is a large area where players can explore without being forced down a certain path. They are able to interact with the environment to differing degrees depending on the game. They may be able to drive cars, buy from shops, jump into a helicopter, dig underground or many other possibilities. This is in contrast to games that force the users down specific routes, into predetermined missions or quests. Open worlds include games such as *Minecraft*, *Grand Theft Auto* and *The Elder Scrolls: Skyrim*.

More than 3 billion people worldwide play video games (Statista, 2024). The global video gaming market has grown rapidly in recent years and the rise of mobile gaming has had a big influence on that. In fact, as of 2022, 45 per cent of video gaming revenue worldwide came from smartphone games. The pandemic was also responsible for the market's growth as consumers sought new ways to pass the time during lockdowns. The data reflects this; for example, the US gaming market (one of the biggest worldwide) reached a record-breaking value of $41.7 billion in 2022 (Statista, 2023a).

Another angle to consider is how the demographics of gamers have changed over time. Over the last decade or so, the percentage of the UK's population between the ages of 55 and 64 that play games has increased from 28 per cent (in 2013) to 41 per cent (in 2022). For the age bracket 45–54, the percentage of gamers rose from 43 per cent to 54 per cent, while for ages 35–44, the increase was from 45 per cent to a huge majority of 67 per cent (Statista, 2023b). This change is reflected in other markets. For example, consumers aged 35–64 now make up 26 per cent of all video game users in the US (Chang, 2024).

These figures tell us that more of society understands and uses games than ever before and therefore we, as marketers, need to understand them so we can understand how our customers interact with the platforms they use today and adapt our platforms to feel comfortable and familiar to them.

Before we continue, it's worth noting that the terms 'gamification' and 'game mechanics' are not interchangeable, but they are closely related. Gamification is the broader concept of applying game-like principles to non-game contexts to motivate and engage users, while game mechanics are the specific tools, techniques and processes within games that make them engaging. Examples of these mechanics include points, levels, badges, challenges, leaderboards, rewards and feedback.

Gamification is already widely used in marketing and manifests as reward schemes, referral programmes and so on. In Web 3.0, however, gaming itself (and not just gamification) will take on a more prominent role in marketing than it does right now.

Gaming in Web 3.0

Virtual goods, currencies and economies have existed for years within games, so the rise of games that involve cryptocurrencies and NFTs is no surprise. One key difference now is that real-world value can be assigned to in-game assets and traded using blockchain technology. For example, in games like *Counter-Strike: Global Offensive*, players have skins that can be sold on third-party marketplaces for real-world money and this real-world value proposition can drive players to invest more in in-game items.

There are a few types of in-game transactions to be aware of. Microtransactions are small purchases that cover cosmetic items like character skins, or functional items like weapons, power-ups or new levels. Next, there are expansion packs – larger content additions that typically add significant new gameplay elements, stories, areas or features. Finally, loot boxes are a type of microtransaction where players purchase a virtual item without knowing what's inside until it's opened. Concerns about the ethics of loot boxes, especially in relation to younger players, have led to discussions about regulations and some countries have already started treating them as a form of gambling.

As games become more sophisticated, there are more ways to create an immersive experience (a principle we'll revisit throughout this chapter) and such experiences help to increase brand awareness and loyalty. One way in which users become immersed is through the narrative; many people are drawn to games because of compelling stories and characters that evoke strong emotional connections, so by understanding the power of storytelling in games, marketers can harness similar techniques to craft more impactful brand narratives.

We must also consider community building. Modern games, especially online multiplayer titles, excel at building and nurturing communities. As Web 3.0 focuses heavily on community-driven platforms and decentralized networks, gleaning lessons from existing gaming communities can be invaluable for marketers aiming to foster brand communities.

Decentralized gaming

As you know, decentralization is a key tenet of Web 3.0, so it's no surprise that gaming is also becoming decentralized. These new types of games are not hosted on a central server but in a distributed manner using blockchain technology.

This new era of gaming provides transparency, democracy and a two-way exchange of value, where players can actually be rewarded financially for participating in and succeeding at games. There are also gaming decentralized autonomous organizations (DAOs), which assign the ownership of a game to all members of the community – players, developers, traders and investors. In gaming DAOs, changes to the gaming process are made as a result of voting (which is managed by smart contracts); decisions are not made by any central authority.

Another key attribute of decentralized games is their interoperability, where assets or identities from one platform might be used or recognized in another, allowing for a more connected and cohesive user experience across different virtual spaces.

Gaming and the metaverse

The metaverse is fertile ground for immersive game experiences that make users feel as though they're inside, or part of, a digital world rather than just passive observers. As the metaverse evolves, game mechanics will be widely employed to enhance user engagement, promote participation and incentivize behaviours. So, instead of merely navigating websites or watching videos, consumers will interact with environments, earn rewards, complete challenges or collaborate with others in game-like scenarios. Marketers must therefore understand game mechanics and interactions to effectively navigate and position their brands in these new worlds. As well as brands creating their own game-like experiences, there is broad scope for product placement within existing games.

The concept of open worlds has been around for some time and the metaverse takes it to new levels. Open world games such as *Skyrim* and *Minecraft* allow players to freely explore the environment and go to any area at any time, without having to follow a predefined path. Metaverse games allow even more freedom; users can create their own virtual worlds with virtual land and real-estate, using cryptocurrency for transactions. *Decentraland* is an example of such a platform; it features what is known as LAND, an NFT for virtual land ownership, and MANA, the cryptocurrency used to purchase LAND and other assets.

Understanding how users interact with games

As games become an integral part of our culture, understanding the psychological reasons behind why and how people interact with them offers invaluable insights for marketers. One area to understand is the intrinsic and extrinsic motivations that drive people during gameplay. While games can bring tangible, extrinsic rewards such as points or digital currency, they also tap into intrinsic motivations – the desire for mastery, to win, to be the first and so on. Understanding these factors helps marketers to craft campaigns and messaging that resonate with an audience's core desires, leading to deeper engagement.

Games are adept at releasing dopamine, a neurotransmitter associated with pleasure and reward, through carefully crafted reward systems (that motivate via extrinsic and intrinsic drives). Recognizing how games achieve this can help marketers design reward-driven campaigns that maintain user engagement and drive specific actions, and understanding gamification principles is key here. Again, I'll be talking about gamification in detail in Chapter 11, but to give a brief example, let's consider risk-and-reward dynamics. Games often create situations where players weigh risks against potential rewards and this decision-making process is intricate. For marketers, understanding this can lead to the creation of campaigns that leverage similar decision-making scenarios, guiding consumer behaviour.

Another key to understanding game interaction is the principle of commitment and investment. Gamers invest time and resources to achieve game objectives and this commitment can be attributed to the sunk cost fallacy, where they continue playing because of the investment they've already made. Marketers can therefore craft strategies that encourage incremental commitment and investment from consumers. It's important here to avoid creating a pay-to-play mechanic where only those that pay can have success. This, while generating revenue from some users, creates resentment among many and stunts long-term growth.

Games provide the opportunity to fulfil another fundamental drive: belonging to a community. In multiplayer games, players often form bonds through collaboration or competing against other communities. We know that fostering a strong community around a brand or product can lead to higher advocacy, organic growth and user-generated content, so again, gaming ties in perfectly with this objective. When designing multiplayer games, it's important to consider social dynamics: namely, interaction, collaboration and competition. Studying these interactions can help marketers to grasp how social dynamics influence decisions, helping in devising community-driven marketing strategies.

Experiences within games

The game experience can be multifaceted, spanning from the immersion in rich storylines and virtual worlds to the thrill of competition. In this section, we'll look more deeply at the different types of game experiences that users seek out.

To start with, let's revisit the concept of immersion and narrative experiences. Many people engage with games as a form of escapism, seeking alternate realities where they can live out different identities or experiences, and narrative-driven games provide the opportunity to do so.

Story-driven gameplay and world-building are two types of gaming that immerse players in deep storylines; the former does so through complex characters and emotional journeys while the latter involves creating expansive worlds with rich lore, histories, cultures and ecosystems. Exploring these worlds is an experience in itself, often independent of the main storyline. Again, virtual reality makes new levels of immersion and creativity possible, while AR games like *Pokémon GO* merge digital and physical worlds, allowing players to interact with game elements in real-world settings.

Next, we have the competitive experiences of player vs player games which pit players against each other in competitive environments. The adrenaline, strategy and team dynamics make PvP experiences both intense and rewarding. Meanwhile, some games focus more on cooperative social experiences where players must work together to achieve goals, complete quests or build intricate structures, *World of Warcraft* and *Minecraft* being classic examples.

Other games provide an opportunity for skill mastery and achievement. These include games that challenge players' cognitive abilities, requiring strategic planning, foresight and problem-solving skills. Many games feature achievement systems that reward players for accomplishing specific tasks, adding an additional layer of goals and milestones to chase. These types of games provide skill mastery and also have applications in educational or self-development contexts, giving players a purpose beyond entertainment. A few examples include language-learning games; mindfulness and relaxation games that offer tranquil environments, promoting relaxation, introspection and even meditation; and therapeutic games used to help with physical rehabilitation, for example.

To sum up, the experiences within games are vast, varied and continually evolving. As technology advances and societal attitudes towards games mature, we're witnessing a medium that offers not just entertainment but profound, meaningful and diverse experiences that can complement and enhance our real-world experiences.

Games becoming brands

These days, it's not just products or services that establish brands; games are becoming brands in and of themselves. Look at phenomena like *Fortnite* or *Minecraft* – these aren't just games anymore, they've evolved into colossal brand entities that captivate global audiences. Individuals don't just play these games – they live in them, investing many hours and forming communities. The trajectory suggests that brands of the future won't simply exist as they do today, they'll cultivate ecosystems. And what's more interactive and immersive than a game-like experience? Marketing is no longer just about selling a product, it's about crafting an experience, a journey, an adventure.

Of course, this does not mean that every company will have to market itself through games, but it's important for marketers to keep an eye on this trend and consider whether they could develop game-like experiences or use techniques inspired by games to create the immersive experiences that consumers are looking for these days.

Also consider how consumers invest in brands by investing time and resources in games. For example, when players purchase tokenized in-game assets that have real-world value, they're investing in the game's brand. Promotions, partnerships or branded content within games can therefore have tangible value beyond traditional advertising approaches. In addition, the relationship between consumers and brands is becoming more symbiotic and this will be reflected in the game experience. In other words, players are no longer just consumers, they're stakeholders, and when they purchase assets that carry genuine real-world value, they're putting their faith in the game's brand. Thus, integrating promotions, partnerships or brand-centric content within games could yield dividends beyond those of traditional advertising.

It's not just about a game's developers or its marketers anymore. The community is a collaborator, a stakeholder, a brand ambassador. While this may be a challenging change of perspective, it will be an opportunity – can you imagine harnessing the raw, unfiltered energy of a game's community for campaigns, events or even product development?

Conclusion

As we move into the era of Web 3.0, games are no longer just platforms for play – they're burgeoning digital societies with their economies, cultures and brand opportunities. Understanding their mechanics and their appeal can provide a competitive edge in crafting campaigns, especially campaigns that are compatible with the metaverse and its immersive experiences. As Web 3.0 ushers in the era of decentralized gaming, marketers will need to recalibrate their strategies, embracing new monetization models and crafting narratives around player empowerment and ownership.

And finally, a challenge. Whether you enjoy gaming or not, I encourage you to try out the following games and aim to really understand them. I hope you enjoy them, but remember, this is not for entertainment – this is for research!

Fortnite

Minecraft

World of Warcraft

Red Dead Redemption 2

Roblox

Enjoy!

Notes

Chang, J (2024) 51 Significant video game demographic statistics: 2024 data on age & gender. FinancesOnline. 4 February, https://financesonline.com/video-game-demographic-statistics/ (archived at https://perma.cc/45G2-6QBE)

Statista (2023a) Mobile gaming market in the United States – statistics & facts. 18 December, www.statista.com/topics/1906/mobile-gaming/#topicOverview (archived at https://perma.cc/GE3J-TACF)

Statista (2023b) Gaming penetration in the United Kingdom (UK) from 2013 to 2022, by age group and gender. 18 August, www.statista.com/statistics/300513/gaming-by-demographic-group-uk (archived at https://perma.cc/GX6Y-88S6)

Statista (2024) Number of video game users worldwide from 2017 to 2027. 9 February, www.statista.com/statistics/748044/number-video-gamers-world/ (archived at https://perma.cc/U2BS-2MWS)

6

Technology foundations

A little advance warning. This chapter is quite technology heavy. Of course, technology is vital as we look to the future of the internet, but I know that not every marketer has strong knowledge of the underlying tech. All the same, I encourage you to read this chapter to understand the timelines and constraints to delivering your Web3 marketing strategy. I have done my best to keep the language detailed enough without being unnecessarily technical.

The possibilities in Web3 are very exciting, but the fact is that currently we're not able to deliver on all of these. While there is no doubt that the technology will be ready, it will be some time before some of the opportunities will reach the realm of the possible. For example, a substantially greater volume of data will be sent per millisecond than ever before, including 3D graphics and high-definition textures, requiring a constant and fast data-transfer rate. To implement this on the scale that many are envisioning demands more advanced solutions than we have right now. This chapter will take an in-depth look at how our current networks fare in terms of supporting Web3, along with some other technologies that need to develop if this new era of the internet is going to materialize at scale.

Bandwidth requirements for Web3

The current speed of data transfer via fibre optic cables is incredibly fast (approaching the speed of light). However, maintaining large visual worlds like metaverses that work for everyone simultaneously poses a range of challenges that can't be overcome through fast data transmission alone. While fibre optic cables provide high bandwidth, there is a finite limit to how much data can be transmitted at once. As the number of users in a metaverse increases, so does the demand for bandwidth, so if too many users are active at the same time, it leads to congestion, slowing down the transfer rates for everyone.

To put it in concrete terms, let's compare the bitrates for different applications (Credit Suisse, 2021):

- web browsing: 1 Mbps
- video streaming (4K): 25 Mbps
- AR: up to 50 Mbps
- high-end VR: 200 Mbps
- holograms: 300 Mbps.

When data travels long distances, the resulting delay, or latency, affects synchronization and real-time interaction. It also causes long loading times, which could make it difficult to explore virtual worlds. When we consider the volume and type of data that would be transmitted in order for the metaverse to function, latency becomes a bigger issue compared with how it affects us today. (It's not just VR that's demanding in terms of bandwidth; the demand caused by Bitcoin and Ethereum transactions is also growing steadily.)

Jitter is the variability in delay between data packets sent over a network; in other words, it's the irregularity with which packets arrive at their destination. In a perfect scenario, packets would arrive at evenly spaced intervals, but due to varying network congestion, route changes and other factors, they might arrive with delays that fluctuate. Again, this is most noticeable and problematic in real-time communications. For services like VoIP, video calls or online gaming, high jitter results in choppy audio or video, unexpected pauses or a decrease in the quality of the call. For streaming applications, it can cause buffering and uneven streaming quality, leading to a poor user experience. In gaming, it can affect gameplay through lagging or jarring movements, which is detrimental in a scenario where timing and position updates are crucial.

As the number of concurrent users increases, the network needs to maintain low and stable latency and jitter to handle the additional load without degrading performance. This is essential for the metaverse to operate on a global scale. The metaverse relies on users being able to interact with the environment and each other in real-time, but high latency can result in slow response times, breaking the illusion of immersion and making the experience less engaging. The disrupted synchronization of shared experiences leads to a disjointed and frustrating user experience, especially in collaborative or competitive scenarios, and sporadic lags and speed-ups can even cause motion sickness in VR environments.

The servers that process the data for metaverses also have limitations. They must handle complex tasks like rendering graphics, managing user interactions and ensuring the physics of the virtual world operate correctly. With a large number of concurrent users, the computational load can overwhelm the servers, regardless of how quickly the data reaches them. In addition, the end-user's equipment, such as their computer, VR headset or other devices used to access the metaverse, may not be able to process the incoming data quickly enough, leading to a bottleneck at the user end of the connection.

Another challenge is the scalability of blockchain networks. The risk of congestion here lies in the fact that every node must process and validate every transaction. Various techniques are being implemented to overcome this challenge, such as sharding. Sharding involves splitting the blockchain network into smaller sub-networks which process a subset of the transactions. Other solutions include replacing proof-of-work (PoW) algorithms with proof-of-stake (PoS) algorithms; essentially, the latter requires simpler computations and is therefore faster and consumes less energy.

The need for infrastructure investment

Fibre cables, compared to their predecessors (such as copper), were revolutionary in terms of increasing network speeds and minimizing delay and jitter. As mentioned, however, the demand of Web3 will outstrip the capabilities of our existing infrastructure. Currently, networks use techniques like jitter buffers to counteract the issues discussed above. A jitter buffer temporarily stores arriving packets in order to counteract delay variation and to have them sent to the application in evenly spaced intervals, thus smoothing out the data flow. However, this can introduce a small amount of delay itself, which is typically a worthwhile trade-off to avoid the negative effects of jitter in real-time communications, but further investment is required in order to upgrade and maintain the networks of the future.

In developed countries, improvements could involve upgrading existing networks to the latest standards, such as fibre to the home (FTTH), as seen in the UK where the old PSTN network is currently being replaced. Newer technologies like 5G will also be deployed; however, 5G is not enough in its current state and new standards need to be developed for mobile access in Web3 (Alriksson et al., 2021).

There will also be investment in edge computing infrastructures that bring data processing closer to the end-user, reducing the distance data needs to travel, thereby decreasing latency. (This is also important for reducing energy consumption, another challenge that Web3 brings.)

For developing economies, the challenge is more foundational. Many regions still lack access to reliable high-speed internet, making the infrastructure leap to support the metaverse more of a quantum one. Investment in these regions must cover not only the deployment of fibre networks but also the broader telecommunications ecosystem, including data centres and the power infrastructure required to ensure network stability.

In areas with geographical challenges, such as extensive rural areas or difficult terrain, the deployment of traditional wired connectivity solutions is not always feasible. Here, investment may need to focus on satellite internet and other technologies that can bridge the gap where laying cables is not practical. All in all, the global disparity in digital infrastructure suggests a future where the experience of Web3 could be vastly different from one region to another.

The need for more powerful hardware

Web3 technologies bring an implicit demand for more robust computing power at the consumer level, so this shift is set to challenge the status quo. Most people currently operate with computers and mobile devices optimized for office work and general use – typically equipped with just enough processing power to run day-to-day applications such as web browsers, office suites and light media-editing tools.

In contrast, various applications we'll find in Web3 demand high-performance computing. In terms of the metaverse, it will be akin to what's currently required for professional gaming, advanced video editing or 3D rendering. Computers will need high-end GPUs capable of rendering detailed virtual environments in real-time and powerful CPUs that can manage the complex simulations and physics of immersive virtual worlds. Greater amounts of RAM will enable smoother multitasking and quicker data access, which are crucial for complex virtual interactions.

Similarly, mobile devices must rise above the standard specifications to accommodate the detailed graphics and persistent connectivity that metaverse interactions require. Efficient battery technology will be pivotal as the metaverse will demand more power to sustain longer periods of use without the need for frequent recharging.

As we venture into the era of Web3, the onus will be on hardware manufacturers to provide consumers with affordable but powerful devices. Meanwhile, software developers will need to optimize platforms to be as resource-efficient as possible to ensure they are accessible to a wider audience without requiring top-of-the-line hardware.

VR advancements for user comfort

For VR technology to become truly mainstream and integrated into daily life, it must overcome several barriers related to user comfort and health. Currently, VR can cause headaches, eye strain or motion sickness, often referred to as 'VR sickness'. To achieve widespread adoption, these issues will need to be addressed to ensure that the majority of people can use VR technology.

As mentioned, low latency is necessary to prevent motion sickness and disorientation. Other measures include designing experiences that minimize abrupt motions or extreme accelerations. VR headsets must also be light enough to wear comfortably for extended periods and they should have adjustable straps, interpupillary distance (IPD) settings and cushioning to fit a variety of head shapes and sizes. Improving the display quality and optimizing refresh rates to reduce flicker are also important considerations.

Interoperability

INTEROPERABILITY

This term refers to the ability of computers to exchange information in a way that enables them all to use it effectively.

The promise of Web3 is a seamlessly connected digital world, but achieving this requires different systems to communicate and collaborate across various platforms and devices. Interoperability is not just a technical challenge but also a conceptual one. For instance, if a system developed for one health service provider needs to work with another for a seamless patient experience, they must understand each other's data formats, privacy protocols and decision-making processes. Another example is in financial services, where interoperability facilitates transactions across different platforms and currencies. A user might want to transfer funds from a bank account to a mobile wallet, or from a cryptocurrency wallet to a traditional investment account. Interoperability ensures these transactions are smooth and secure, providing a unified experience regardless of the platforms involved.

To achieve such interoperability, there needs to be a set of agreed-upon standards and protocols that allow different systems to communicate effectively. These standards must be adopted by device manufacturers, software developers and service providers. Proper governance models will also need to be in place to manage and update these standards as technology evolves.

AI concerns

As Web3 matures, the role of AI will be pivotal, but so too will be the vigilance with which we address the concerns around it. With AI-driven systems becoming more adept at handling complex tasks, they also become attractive targets for cybercriminals. These criminals can exploit AI in various ways that lead to sophisticated and persistent cyber-attacks. AI can analyse patterns to breach systems in ways humans might not anticipate and the arms race between security professionals and cybercriminals could escalate to unprecedented levels.

There is also the threat of adversarial AI, where systems are deceived into making erroneous decisions or predictions. Adversarial AI involves techniques where AI systems are manipulated through deceptive inputs, also known as 'poisoning'. These techniques are most commonly associated with the field of machine learning, and especially with the subfield of deep learning. An attacker feeds the deceptive data into a machine learning model so that it will make a mistake; this often involves subtle perturbations to data that are imperceptible or seem irrelevant to humans. However, it can lead AI systems to misclassify or misinterpret the data. For example, changing a few pixels in an image in a way that's undetectable to the human eye can cause an image-recognition system to mislabel it.

Adversarial AI has significant implications as it can fool systems that make critical decisions, such as those used for autonomous vehicles, medical purposes, facial recognition and malware detection. There's also the threat of hackers stealing sensitive information that's used as training data.

In response to this threat, researchers are working on developing defences. These include adversarial training, where a model is trained on a mixture of normal and adversarial examples. In addition, there's input sanitization, where inputs are cleaned to remove potential adversarial noise. There are also techniques for making models less sensitive to small perturbations in their input.

Manipulation can also affect the integrity of smart contracts. Yes, the terms of a smart contract are agreed in advance by the parties involved and encoded into the contract. Under normal circumstances, once a smart contract is deployed, its terms should be immutable. This is one of the key value propositions of blockchain technology and smart contracts, since it provides a trustless environment where parties can be confident that the contract will execute exactly as written. However, there are scenarios in which manipulation can take place. Many smart contracts rely on external information such as price feeds or the results of events. If manipulated data is provided, the smart contract will still execute based on this data, potentially leading to undesired outcomes. (There is a theoretical future risk that advancements in quantum computing could allow an entity to break the cryptographic assurances of a blockchain and alter smart contracts. However, this is more speculative and not currently a practical concern (Davis and Kim, 2023).)

Another challenge surrounding AI is accountability. Web3 promises greater user governance and less central control, which can also mean decentralized AI systems that operate autonomously. Ensuring these systems are accountable and that the decisions they make are transparent and fair is a significant challenge. This lack of clarity becomes a problem in critical situations, such as when a system is responsible for a car accident or a healthcare mishap. The 'black box' nature of AI systems – particularly deep-learning models – exacerbates this as it can be difficult to interpret how an AI reached a particular conclusion. As these systems become more autonomous, the need for accountability and explainability becomes more urgent in order to manage risk.

The rapid pace of AI development means it often outstrips the slower processes of regulatory adaptation. This lag can lead to periods in which AI activities exist in a grey area, without clear guidelines or protections. Also, AI's global nature doesn't respect national borders, making jurisdiction and enforcement of regulations a complex issue. As Web3 aims to be a decentralized platform, traditional regulatory approaches may not be sufficient or appropriate. The development of new, adaptive regulatory frameworks that can evolve with AI technology will be crucial to mitigate risks without stifling innovation.

Conclusion

In summary, we have a long way to go before we can fully embrace Web3 on a global scale. Our current infrastructure just isn't advanced enough. There's also a lot of work to do when it comes to security and AI comes with ethical concerns that have no easy solution. Speaking of ethics, I'll be talking about that more in the next chapter.

Notes

Alriksson, F, Ho Kang, D, Phillips, C, Pradas, J L and Zaidi, A (2021) XR and 5G: Extended reality at scale with time-critical communication. 24 August, www.ericsson.com/en/reports-and-papers/ericsson-technology-review/articles/xr-and-5g-extended-reality-at-scale-with-time-critical-communication (archived at https://perma.cc/BQC3-9SPQ)

Credit Suisse (2021) Metaverse: A guide to the Next-Gen internet. www.credit-suisse.com/media/assets/corporate/docs/about-us/media/media-release/2022/03/metaverse-14032022.pdf (archived at https://perma.cc/24ER-YTU7)

Davis, D and Kim, A (2023) Quantum Computing Could Threaten Blockchain, Crypto. Bloomberg Law. 17 August, https://news.bloomberglaw.com/us-law-week/quantum-computing-could-threaten-blockchain-crypt (archived at https://perma.cc/ZH9K-J58X)

7

Ethics and marketing in Web 3.0

Decentralized networks, blockchain technology and a strong emphasis on anonymity pave the way for better user experiences on the whole. However, this progress brings forth ethical challenges, primarily due to the reduced role of centralized authorities in monitoring and regulating online spaces. Does this sound familiar? Does it remind you of the dark web at all? I'm not suggesting that Web 3.0 will lead to a swathe of platforms enabling the types of crimes the dark web is associated with, but considering its decentralized structure, the lines could blur if we're not careful.

The dark web is infamous for hosting content and activities that are illegal or ethically dubious. With Web 3.0's emphasis on user-controlled experiences and reduced censorship, there's a risk that without effective moderation, it could inadvertently host or facilitate similar types of content, such as extremist propaganda or illegal marketplaces. Both the dark web and Web 3.0 place a high value on user anonymity and yes, this protects user privacy and freedoms, but it also opens the door to misuse, so it's important to implement proper safeguards as soon as possible.

Cryptocurrencies are another common element that underpins both domains. They facilitate private financial transactions but also can be used for money laundering, illicit purchases and other illegal activities. If the regulations are not kept up to date or communities are not adequately monitored, Web 3.0 could see a rise in activities that mirror dark web practices. Of course, governments worldwide have been grappling with the regulation of cryptocurrency in recent years, which included the evolution of Anti-Money Laundering (AML) and Know Your Customer (KYC) laws. These laws require cryptocurrency exchanges and wallets to verify the identity of their users, helping prevent money laundering and the financing of terrorism by making it more difficult for criminals to use cryptocurrencies anonymously.

As cryptocurrency becomes more mainstream in the future, regulators will need to overcome several obstacles. One of the biggest challenges is balancing the need to protect consumers and prevent illegal activities with the desire to foster innovation and the growth of the cryptocurrency market. In addition, the rapid pace of technological change in cryptocurrencies means that regulations can quickly become outdated and will require continuous monitoring and adaptation. Also, achieving a global consensus on how to regulate cryptocurrencies is challenging, given the varying legal and economic frameworks across countries.

To reiterate, this new era of the internet requires a renewed commitment to ethical practices and user safety due to the increased risks (and variety of risks) involved. There's already a lack of adequate protection for vulnerable individuals on the internet and since marketing in Web 3.0 is very community-focused, the platforms enabling those communities need to be responsible for user well-being. Throughout this chapter I'll talk about some of the threats facing different populations and what needs to be done to protect them.

Vulnerable populations and risks in Web3

Women and children often face heightened risks of exposure to harmful content and online abuse, while the mental health consequences of spending too much time on Web 3.0 – or being exposed to the wrong types of content – are varied. We also have to think about how we target consumers, as the heightened potential for targeted marketing can be a double-edged sword. On the one hand, it allows for highly personalized consumer experiences; on the other, it can lead to exploitative practices, particularly towards vulnerable groups. Marketers have a responsibility to ensure that their strategies do not inadvertently harm these groups and this includes avoiding manipulative tactics that prey on insecurities and being mindful of the mental and emotional impacts of marketing campaigns.

Protecting children and women

The concerns surrounding the protection of children from the threats of Web 3.0 are multifaceted. A central issue is the exposure of children to inappropriate or harmful content; decentralized platforms may lack the centralized content-moderation systems typical of Web 2.0, potentially leading to increased exposure to content that is not age-appropriate, such as violence, pornography or extremist ideologies. Ensuring robust and effective content moderation in a decentralized environment is a significant challenge, which I'll talk about more shortly.

Children are also particularly vulnerable to privacy risks as they may not fully understand the implications of handing over their data. While Web 3.0 promises greater user privacy in some aspects, the rise in IoT applications, especially those that collect biometric data, may present problems and once biometric data is out in the open, it's too late – it can't be changed like a leaked password can. Children are an important segment for businesses considering the influence they have on household spending, so it's going to be important to develop robust security measures for these types of applications.

The lack of effective oversight inherent in a decentralized internet, along with the increased potential for anonymous interactions, may lead to an increase in activities such as cyberbullying and harassment, with children being particularly susceptible to these threats. There's also the risk of grooming and exploitation, as predators may find it easier to interact with children in environments where identity verification is lax or non-existent.

Another consideration is the effects that excessive VR use may have on brain and eye development. Manufacturers place age restrictions on

VR headsets and this may be because there is not enough data on their effects. With that said, some scientists have commented that prolonged use of improperly fitted devices could cause damage to a developing brain (Scientific American, 2016).

Research conducted in collaboration with the Italian Institute of Technology indicates that VR could potentially disrupt motor development. In virtual environments, children use a different coordination strategy compared with in real life. ('Coordination strategy' refers to the importance given to different sensory inputs such as vision and proprioception and how they all work together to control movement.) In the study, children assigned more importance to vision in VR than they would naturally. It was also revealed that head–trunk coordination is not mature at age 10, let alone at age eight, the age at which it was previously assumed to be developed fully (Sanctuary, 2021).

The effects that VR has on psychological development is another cause for concern. For example, prolonged exposure to a virtual environment could limit the individual's ability to discern fiction from reality; by default, young children are not always able to do so anyway and VR could exacerbate that, interfering with normal developmental processes. Any content that could be considered traumatic would also have a more profound effect in VR compared with when watching a film, which again highlights the importance of having appropriate controls for age-restricted content (Scientific American, 2016).

Like the ethical concerns affecting children, those affecting women are not entirely new but are amplified in the Web 3.0 environment. For example, women often face gender-based harassment, stalking, catfishing and other forms of abuse online and decentralization makes it more challenging to track and penalize abusive behaviour. In addition, cryptocurrencies can facilitate illegal activities such as exploitation and human trafficking, crimes that disproportionately affect women.

Addressing all of these concerns requires a concerted effort from tech companies, policymakers, educators, and parents. Solutions include developing new technologies for safer content moderation, establishing global standards for child safety in Web 3.0, enhancing digital literacy and education for both children and parents, and creating more effective legal frameworks to protect women and young users in a decentralized digital world.

Web 3.0 and mental health

The metaverse may be especially troublesome for individuals with mental health difficulties, the immersive experiences involved potentially leading to increased screen time and addiction. The compelling, gamified nature of these interactive environments might make it difficult for some users to disengage, potentially causing compulsive use, which can affect sleep, physical health and daily functioning.

Gaming as we know it today is already a problem for some users and can become an addiction for many. This is something that many parents will agree is something they need to control carefully. When we add the fully immersive experiences promised by the metaverse into the equation, it could exacerbate this issue – not just for gamers but for anyone with a propensity towards addictive behaviour or escapism.

In the last chapter I mentioned how brands will start to create game-like ecosystems that customers may spend a lot of time using. So, going back to the role of marketing in all of this, it's going to be important to find ways to protect users from addictive behaviour when creating immersive branded experiences. As it stands, social media is a drain on many people's time; however, the platforms want to maximize the time users spend on there in order to profit. If metaverse platforms are going to fail their users in the same way social media has, then it will be down to brands to implement protective features into their own ecosystems. These may include warnings, reminders to take breaks, automatic pauses that will help users remember to take breaks, as well as user guides that provide suggestions for balanced use.

Education should extend to recognizing signs of addiction and understanding the importance of time spent outside of virtual environments.

Once again, it's difficult to determine who's responsible for educating consumers of a decentralized service but at the very least, parents and employers should be well informed of the warning signs in order to protect adolescents and employees from overuse, respectively.

It's not only addiction we need to be concerned about when it comes to VR. I mentioned earlier that there's a risk of children developing altered perceptions of reality due to the impact of highly interactive and realistic content, so it's just as well that there are age restrictions on VR headsets. However, it's not only children that are affected by this phenomenon. VR could affect adolescents and adults in a similar way, as demonstrated in a 2022 study, 'Virtual reality induces symptoms of depersonalization and derealization: A longitudinal randomised control trial' (Peckmann et al., 2022). Depersonalization and derealization are forms of dissociation, the former being when someone feels that they are outside of themselves, observing themselves; the latter is the sense that the world itself is unreal. The study showed that symptoms of both were experienced after PC and VR gaming, the effects being much stronger with VR. The symptoms were temporary, but nobody knows for sure what the long-term consequences might be of repeated experience. There are a lot of unknowns when it comes to the psychological and neurological effects of VR and that is why we need to proceed with caution (Peckmann et al., 2022).

Many studies have shown that excessive social media use can lead to feelings of inadequacy and loneliness and may trigger or exacerbate anxiety, depression, eating disorders and other conditions. Web 3.0 may make this worse; despite offering new ways to connect, some users might prefer and grow accustomed to the controlled interactions in virtual spaces, so instead of real-world socializing, they may have fewer face-to-face interactions and a greater sense of loneliness or isolation than they would otherwise.

Over the years, several well-known cases have been discussed in the news where individuals with heavy social media use developed eating disorders and died due to the medical consequences or suicide. Constant comparison to others is unhealthy, but with social media use, this way of thinking is unavoidable – unless, of course, the individual uses the platforms for their most basic functions such as messaging and finding events – and that's not what the metaverse is about. With VR, issues relating to body image and self-esteem could potentially get worse because it provides an intensified version of what people experience through social media.

Some campaigners have suggested that social media should display a warning in the same way a packet of cigarettes does. In fact, the Royal Society for Public Health recommended that these platforms display warnings about 'heavy usage' after the user has spent a certain amount of time on them (Royal Society for Public Health, May 2017).

Responsible marketing practices in Web 3.0

Community platforms will be responsible for setting and enforcing ethical standards. As such, marketers can foster positive, safe online spaces by creating content that upholds community values, actively engaging with community feedback to ensure respectful marketing and using data ethically to enhance user experiences without crossing the line by exploiting vulnerabilities. One of the keys to achieving this is building trust within communities, which also makes it easier for newcomers to distinguish between a safe community and one with malicious intent. Transparent marketing practices, such as clear disclosure of sponsored content and honest representation of products and services, will continue to be crucial in building trust.

In the UK, the communications regulator Ofcom has published new guidelines for complying with the Online Safety Act. The Act requires that the types of online services within its remit take measures to protect users from illegal activity and illegal content, including child sexual abuse material, material encouraging suicide or self-harm, terrorism, sales of illegal drugs or weapons, and fraud. The types of online services that will need to comply include search engines, platforms that host user-generated content such as social media sites, messaging services and video-sharing platforms. There are plans to introduce new online safety regulations in the US in 2024 and this is likely to be reflected in other jurisdictions.

As I said in the last chapter, AI has its ethical drawbacks, but there are applications in which it has a lot to offer in terms of safety. For example, AI models can monitor content and identify the presence of anything illegal or explicit, flagging it to be removed before users see it. This is necessary because of the rise of user-generated content; no human moderators will be able to keep up with it all in the future. Through NLP, abusive language can be detected and perpetrators can be penalized. AI systems may also flag repeated offences, even if the account has not been reported, leading to restricted access. A challenge here will be defining what constitutes abuse and avoiding infringing on freedom of expression.

Conclusion

Web 3.0 exacerbates many existing threats affecting women, children and individuals with mental health difficulties. There will be new risks to monitor, such as the developmental and psychological effects of overusing VR. If we're going to ensure Web 3.0 remains a force for positive innovation, it's crucial to implement robust ethical guidelines within decentralized communities as well as strong regulatory frameworks and governance models. Stakeholders in the Web 3.0 ecosystem must be vigilant in monitoring and addressing any signs of platforms being used for unethical purposes, preventing them from devolving into anything that resembles the dark web.

As marketers it is vital that we consider all our consumers when we build experiences. It's critical that we own the ethics of our campaigns and we create clear policies for use of data. It's important to consider the technological impacts of our platforms and that we work with regulators to ensure an environment that is functional, fit, fair and free for all to use equally and without worry.

Notes

Peckmann, C, Kannen, K, Pensel, M C, Lux, S, Philipsen, A and Braun, N (2022) Virtual reality induces symptoms of depersonalization and derealization: A longitudinal randomised control trial. ScienceDirect. www.sciencedirect.com/science/article/pii/S0747563222000553 (archived at https://perma.cc/D2F6-RCU3)

Royal Society for Public Health (2017) #StatusofMind. RSPH. www.rsph.org.uk/our-work/campaigns/status-of-mind.html (archived at https://perma.cc/PEC8-87W6)

Sanctuary, H (2021) Virtual reality affects children differently than adults. Neuroscience News. 27 September, https://neurosciencenews.com/virtual-reality-children-19370/ (archived at https://perma.cc/HC9F-WVME)

Scientific American (2016) Are virtual reality headsets safe for children? 4 October, www.scientificamerican.com/article/are-virtual-reality-headsets-safe-for-children/ (archived at https://perma.cc/9WVN-CBCY)

PART TWO

Marketing in Web 2.5

8

The changing face of reality

Virtual reality is not a new concept, the idea has been around for decades. You could even suggest that it has been around as a concept for centuries. It is only in the past 30 years however that technology has existed to make this dream a reality.

In the 1990s this technology was exciting, but in reality (please excuse the pun) it was too basic to be of any practical use. In the 2010s, however, the push of augmented reality with initiatives such as Google Glass and *Pokémon GO* led to a refreshed focus on the platform. Since then, we have seen a wide range of devices, games, experiences and platforms arrive to serve, invest in and bring this technology to market.

VR may (or may not) be important for the future of the metaverse, but beyond the casual user who may want to shoot aliens, walk on the moon or share a meal with family who are based overseas, there are also business cases for training surgeons and emergency response teams, teaching and much more.

A quick look at the numbers

The market, valued at $25.1 billion in 2023, is expected to reach $72.1 billion by 2028 at a compound annual growth rate (CAGR) of 18 per cent (MarketsandMarkets.com, 2022).

The number of global users of AR and VR is expected to reach 6 billion by 2028 and 51 per cent of consumers stated that VR and

AR are the top technologies they want to use to assist them in their daily lives. So far, these technologies have seen the greatest degree of adoption in China and the US. While that figure of 6 billion may seem very high, we should keep in mind that AR has many forms and VR is only starting to enter the mainstream, with the price point of the technology and breadth of the experience still rather limited. This will change over the coming years (Papagiannis, 2020; Statista, 2023).

AR and VR have opened new frontiers in customer experience that transcend traditional marketing boundaries. In this chapter we'll review some case studies on their use. We'll also look at the relationship between VR and the metaverse, as well as the different platforms and frameworks marketers can use to start creating immersive experiences.

How brands are using VR and AR

As I've mentioned, these technologies create novel experiences that captivate customers, fostering a deeper emotional connection with brands. For instance, VR can transport a user to a virtual beach to showcase a travel destination, while AR can bring a static advertisement to life with interactive features. The key lies in their ability to break the physical–digital barrier, offering tactile and engaging experiences that traditional marketing channels cannot provide.

Brands are using these technologies for fun as well as practical purposes and the best experiences offer a balance of both elements. This balance ensures users are engaged while they also receive tangible value, like product information or practical demonstrations. Creating a virtual world that users can interact with in a meaningful way, whether it's exploring a virtual store or customizing products in a virtual space, is crucial in this sense.

The interactive, sensory nature of VR and AR significantly increases customer engagement and this translates into a stronger influence on purchase decisions. New, creative campaigns based on these technologies are appearing all the time, so let's go through a few examples.

Volvo: virtual test drives and mixed-reality showrooms

In 2014, Volvo was set to release its XC90 model and needed a campaign that would inspire engagement while showcasing the vehicle's design and capabilities. Using the VR platform Google Cardboard, Volvo developed an interactive experience it could demonstrate at the LA Auto Show that year. Users downloaded the 'Volvo Reality' app and placed their device in the Google Cardboard mount so they could view the vehicle's interior and have a virtual test drive. Volvo was able to provide the test drive experience by collecting 360-degree environmental data from a drive along a real road and combining it with CGI. The Auto Show was months ahead of the launch date of the new vehicle, making it all the more important to create an experience that would keep the brand in the forefront of consumers' minds.

The technology gives customers the convenience of exploring different vehicles efficiently from their own homes instead of visiting one after the other in person, a time-consuming endeavour that eats into their precious leisure time. Users can also test multiple vehicle models in one sitting, saving yet more time, and dealers benefit from minimizing the costs of keeping vehicles on the premises.

Timmy Ghiurau, Senior Lead XR and Virtual Experiences at the time, said that the VR experience helped the company reach more markets and more journalists, as there are a limited number of physical cars available when a company launches a new model (Rozema, 2024).

Volvo didn't stop at test drives. In 2019, it opened several so-called 'experience stores' in Tokyo, Milan and Stockholm. Customers could test and configure different models within a VR experience, which also featured a storytelling element to explain each model's design and capabilities (Virtual Reality Marketing, 2019). In addition, the company has used AR to enhance the showroom experience, enabling customers to view life-size 3D holograms of the car and its parts. This helps them to really understand each vehicle's features and lets them experience safety features that would not usually be demonstrable in a typical test drive, such as automatic stopping to prevent collisions (Automative News Europe, 2015).

Of course, Volvo is absolutely not the only car manufacturer using VR and AR for sales and marketing purposes. Many companies are using it for marketing, product development and training, while Toyota created a VR experience to raise awareness about safety for teenage drivers.

IKEA's Place app

IKEA didn't want customers to have to rely on guesswork when it came to deciding whether a piece of furniture would look good in their homes and offices. So in 2017 the company launched its Place app – users simply select items of virtual furniture to drop into their homes and view through their phone's camera. The objects are 3D and true to scale – no need to walk around the store with a tape measure anymore or take the risk of buying an item that doesn't fit and having to return it. (According to IKEA, the app scales items with 98 per cent accuracy (IKEA, 2017).)

Customers can also get inspired by testing out different designs and colours which may help them create their overall design plan, and the textures and finer details of each piece are displayed with clarity. Users can move furniture around to see how it looks in different positions in the room – a lot less hassle than moving the real item multiple times. They can also save their designs, share them as photos or video and seamlessly order the products through their local IKEA website.

IKEA has been something of a first-mover in AR; it was one of the first companies to use Apple's AR framework, ARKit, and also experimented with a more primitive version of the app in 2013. Since 2017, it has expanded the Place app's functionality by adding 'Studio Mode', a feature that virtually furnishes walls, ceilings, chairs, table tops and other elements of a room. Users can adjust lighting levels and the 3D models are said to be much more realistic than before (IKEA, 2020).

The Place app is perhaps one of the best examples of using AR for marketing due to the creativity and engagement it inspires. Anyone who is into interior design could spend hours testing different combinations and after investing time in experimenting with it all, are they going to go to a competitor? Unlikely. And the seamless purchase experience is the icing on the cake.

L'Oréal: virtual makeup

This example demonstrates how companies are creating novelty experiences to maintain brand awareness and engagement, as opposed to the more practical examples discussed above. During the pandemic, L'Oréal released a range of AR filters that would allow customers to virtually 'try on' makeup. The filters could be used with social media and video-calling apps, allowing customers to experiment just for fun or to have a break from putting on real makeup during all those Zoom meetings. It also inspired customers to choose L'Oréal when shopping for cosmetics in future. Social media is a vital marketing channel when it comes to cosmetics, with 33 per cent of buyers liking or following a brand on social media, so L'Oréal made a good move here (Statista, 2024).

The virtual makeup filters came about after L'Oréal's acquisition of ModiFace, a software company that develops technology for the beauty industry. ModiFace has created various AR experiences for different makeup brands, as well as virtual hair colouring for Garnier and Color & Co. After sales had dropped 19 per cent during the pandemic, the campaign drove sales of L'Oréal's cosmetics to increase by 30 per cent, e-commerce sales being particularly strong. Similar applications of AR are offered by fashion brands from H&M to Louis Vuitton, letting customers virtually try on clothes.

Nike: sky-high promotion

Another campaign spawned during the pandemic was Nike's promotion of its Air Max 2090s to the Brazilian market using AR. Instead of getting customers to download an app, it created a microsite dedicated to the campaign. Users had to point their phones at the sky in order to find an AR cloud shaped as an Air Max shoe. When they found it, they got access to hip-hop artist Djonga's latest track and music video, as well as other tracks and exclusive interviews with other artists. This is another example of an AR experience that was mostly for fun but served another purpose – promoting the product (Tsirulnik, n.d.).

The sportswear giant has also been creating VR experiences for some time, allowing customers to virtually try on shoes, but it doesn't stop there. Nike even created a metaverse called Nikeland, where customers can further interact with the brand. Nikeland is modelled after the company's headquarters and includes fields and arenas where users can play games and interact with other users, with avatars adorned in Nike apparel. Users can also explore a virtual showroom of Nike products, which contains recent as well as classic releases (Mytaverse, 2022).

AR advertising

AR is transforming advertising by turning passive viewing experiences into interactive ones. This is important because more and more consumers these days are using ad blockers or simply ignoring ads, as they are exposed to so many each day. However, AR brings ads to life and creates experiences that consumers actually want to be a part of. Way back in 2011, the BBC's *Top Gear* magazine used AR to enliven its printed content and saw an engagement rate of 27 per cent and click-through rate (CTR) of 25 per cent as a result. Another example is Burger King's 'Burn That Ad' campaign from 2019. Customers could scan competitors' ads and set them on fire virtually, winning them a free Whopper in the process (Fedko, 2023).

A key advantage of investing in AR ads over VR experiences is that they are easier for consumers to access as in many cases they only need a smartphone.

VR and the metaverse

In 2021, Meta announced that it was developing a new, high-end VR headset nicknamed 'Project Cambria'. It's finally been released under the name Meta Quest Pro and not only is it built to support advanced

VR functionality, but it supports mixed reality as well, allowing users to combine elements of the physical and digital without needing a separate device. But what about people that don't own headsets? Can they still access virtual worlds?

Virtual reality is a fundamental building block of the metaverse, but it is not necessary to use VR in order to experience it. The term 'metaverse' applies to any computer-generated environment where users can interact, so while VR provides a profound depth of immersion, it's not a prerequisite for the metaverse's existence; it's just one of the fundamental technologies behind it.

One of the key differences between the two is that VR experiences do not necessarily happen in a shared space. The metaverse, however, is shared and is persistent – in other words, the virtual world in question is still active while a given user is not connected to it; with VR, the experience ends when the user takes off their headset. Another difference is the fact that the metaverse, in theory, should allow a user to do anything they could do in the real world, virtually. The metaverse is extensive in that way, while VR generally offers prescribed experiences.

Being able to access the metaverse without VR equipment is beneficial for customers that still seek engaging experiences but don't have the budget for headsets or computers with sufficient processing power; in turn, marketers can reach a broader audience this way. In this scenario, users can access platforms with their usual devices and they will still have an avatar through which they interact within the virtual space – they just have a level of separation that VR does not allow.

A few platforms that users can access without VR include *Fortnite*, *The Sandbox* and *VRChat*. As mentioned, *Fortnite* was traditionally a gaming platform but more metaverse features are being added all the time, including live concerts and other events (during which users can interact with each other) and it now has world-building features. *The Sandbox* focuses primarily on world-building and incorporates Ethereum, allowing users to make money from their gaming experiences.

Another option is *Roblox*, which is mostly used for gaming purposes, but brands are also using it to create varied experiences (in fact, Nikeland is built on this platform). Finally, *VRChat* is like a modern-day chatroom where users interact with the community through avatars as well as play games.

Current VR and AR technologies

Microsoft HoloLens is a self-contained, holographic computer built into a headset that enables users to interact with holograms in the world around them. Interaction is carried out using natural gestures and voice commands, offering an intuitive and hands-free experience (HoloLens 2 is the current version; the previous version has been discontinued). This tool has been largely used in industrial applications, but the examples I mentioned earlier (such as examining 3D holograms of car parts) show its potential in consumer-facing scenarios. Developers can build apps for HoloLens through various environments, including DirectX, Unity, Unreal Engine, or buildwagon (for web developers).

I also mentioned Apple's ARKit (used by IKEA) which is designed for building AR experiences into apps and games on iOS devices. It uses the iOS device's camera, processors and motion sensors in order to create interactive experiences and offers advanced face tracking, scene understanding and 3D object-detection features. It can detect surfaces, for example, so that virtual objects can be placed upon them. It also has a multiplayer feature, where different devices can view the same scene, and through its motion-capture and people-occlusion capabilities, it can position AR content in front of or behind people in the user's environment, for a better experience. There's also the Reality Composer tool, enabling users without 3D experience to use an existing library of 3D objects.

Google's AR development platform is called ARCore and it has the same capabilities of ARKit. Another feature that both options have is light estimation; this enables the detection of the light intensity in the physical world and replicates it so that the virtual objects appear under the same conditions, for a more realistic experience.

Meta·offers Spark AR Studio for creating AR experiences for Facebook, Messenger and Instagram. It's user-friendly and offers a range of creative tools, including the option to build AR ads. Just a couple of case studies listed on Spark AR Studio's website include an AR music video by Universal Music UK and an immersive game by airBaltic which led to 2.6 times more conversations and a 51 per cent higher return on advertising spend (ROAS).

Other popular AR development platforms include Vuforia Engine, which supports a wide range of devices, and Wikitude, a framework that specializes in location-based AR and image recognition. It's compatible with various development environments and supports multiple platforms.

As for VR development, Unity 3D is among the most popular options. Most famous for game development, it's now widely used for VR development as well, offering CAD tools and other artist and designed tools. Similarly, Unreal Engine is a popular choice for professional developers and is said to be useful for creating prototypes quickly. The Google VR development portal offers a range of development tools that can be used with various platforms (Davies, n.d.).

For people with no experience developing VR or 3D graphics specifically, Amazon Sumerian could be the way to go. This VR engine from AWS is compatible with a broad range of VR headsets, including Oculus Rift, Oculus Go, HTC Vive, Lenovo Mirage and Google Daydream, as well as iOS and Android devices. There are also several platforms out there, including WebVR, for developing experiences that are accessible from a web browser (Davies, n.d.).

Conclusion

The adoption of VR and AR is increasing at a rapid pace and consumers are coming to expect brands to offer such experiences, especially younger audiences. Many brands have been using these technologies for marketing purposes for more than a decade and we've looked at a range of creative campaigns offering both AR and VR experiences. There are many options for creating these experiences, ranging from tools to create simple AR ads through to fully fledged development environments for building immersive VR experiences.

Looking to the future, trends such as more advanced headsets and increased realism in VR are set to shape the marketing landscape, opening new doors for engagement. We may even see AI-driven personalized VR content that adapts to user preferences and behaviours. For now, however, brands from all walks of life need to start experimenting with these technologies to capture the attention of today's audiences.

Notes

Automative News Europe (2015) Volvo, Microsoft will bring augmented reality into showrooms. 20 November, https://europe.autonews.com/article/20151120/ANE/151129998/volvo-microsoft-will-bring-augmented-reality-into-showrooms (archived at https://perma.cc/UPY7-NWA3)

Davies, A (n.d.) 10 great tools for VR development. www.devteam.space/blog/10-great-tools-for-vr-development/ (archived at https://perma.cc/HXG5-QLAS)

Fedko, D (2023) Top 16 examples of augmented reality ads. Wear Studio. 5 November, https://wear-studio.com/top-examples-of-augmented-reality-ads/ (archived at https://perma.cc/SQ2M-75Y5)

IKEA (2017) IKEA Place app launched to help people virtually place furniture at home. 12 September, www.ikea.com/global/en/newsroom/innovation/ikea-launches-ikea-place-a-new-app-that-allows-people-to-virtually-place-furniture-in-their-home-170912/ (archived at https://perma.cc/9X47-PW3R)

IKEA (2020) New AR capabilities for IKEA Place on iPad Pro. 19 March, www.ikea.com/global/en/newsroom/innovation/ikea-to-launch-new-ar-capabilities-for-ikea-place-on-new-ipad-pro-200319/ (archived at https://perma.cc/NG64-AZTD)

MarketsandMarkets.com (2022) Augmented (AR) and virtual reality (VR) market. October, www.marketsandmarkets.com/Market-Reports/augmented-reality-virtual-reality-market-1185.html (archived at https://perma.cc/L996-A558)

Mytaverse (2022) Nike's metaverse VR experiences are paying off – here's why. 21 October, www.mytaverse.com/post/nike-s-metaverse-vr-experiences-are-paying-off-here-s-why (archived at https://perma.cc/C3JC-VGAU)

Papagiannis, H (2020) How AR is redefining retail in the pandemic. Harvard Business Review. 7 October, https://hbr.org/2020/10/how-ar-is-redefining-retail-in-the-pandemic (archived at https://perma.cc/4T89-CPD4)

Rozema, R (2024) Cutting-edge VR and AR solutions help Volvo Cars attract new customers. www.candidplatform.com/en/news/platform-news/all-platform-news/marketing/cutting-edge-vr-and-ar-solutions-help-volvo-cars-attract-new-customers.html (archived at https://perma.cc/2JEX-6QRN)

Statista (2023) AR & VR – worldwide. www.statista.com/outlook/amo/ar-vr/worldwide (archived at https://perma.cc/HH3L-KEHQ)

Statista (2024) Leading interactions of beauty product buyers with brands on social media worldwide in 1st quarter 2019. July, www.statista.com/statistics/1241980/beauty-brand-interactions-social-world/ (archived at https://perma.cc/7K6B-CEUJ)

Tsirulnik, G (n.d.) Nike, Fanta augmented reality case studies showcased at MMF. Marketing Dive. www.marketingdive.com/ex/mobilemarketer/cms/news/advertising/6515.html (archived at https://perma.cc/X798-GRRT)

Virtual Reality Marketing (2019) Volvo Studios VR Automotive. 23 February, www.virtualrealitymarketing.com/case-studies/volvo-studios-vr/ (archived at https://perma.cc/E498-UP79)

9

Using AI in your marketing

AI is disrupting the marketing industry in profound ways. One of the most well-known examples of this revolution is the rapid growth of OpenAI's ChatGPT, the app that had 500,000 downloads within six days of its launch, becoming the fastest growing platform launch ever. A year later, the total number of installations reached 110 million (Perez, 2023a, 2023b).

However, ChatGPT is just the tip of the iceberg. AI is permeating every aspect of marketing, including market research, SEO, advertising, video creation and much more. In this chapter, we will delve into these use cases and discuss how the roles of marketers are evolving as AI works alongside us.

FIGURE 9.1 The speed of ChatGPT growth (Adapted from Duarte, 2024)

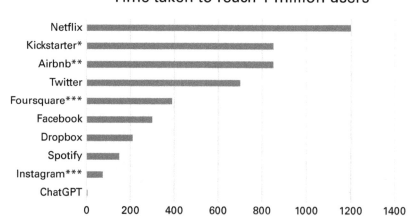

Time taken to reach 1 million users

Generative AI and ChatGPT

Generative AI refers to a subset of artificial intelligence that focuses on generating original, contextually relevant content, based on knowledge learned from large datasets. This content can be in the form of text, images, audio and video. You are likely familiar with ChatGPT by now, an advanced language model that can do everything from write poetry in the style of Shakespeare to generate code. It's also being used to build advanced chatbots for customer service purposes.

Advanced AI-driven chatbots are not just automated responders, they are intelligent conversational agents capable of engaging customers with a human touch. They provide personalized responses, answer queries, recommend products and facilitate the customer journey in a seamless and engaging manner. They can operate around the clock and provide instant responses, leading to enhanced customer satisfaction. They can handle a large volume of inquiries simultaneously (in multiple languages) without the need for additional staff, thus reducing labour costs. As such, they can easily support a growing business, scaling to meet increased demand without the need to hire and train human agents.

ChatGPT can generate content ideas for blogs, social media posts, email campaigns and other marketing materials. Users can provide a topic or a brief description and ChatGPT will suggest interesting angles, trends or related topics to explore. It can also help identify relevant keywords, but since it can't give you information about search volume or any other metrics, it's only worth using as a starting point for SEO. After planning your content, it can help you write it by suggesting SEO-optimized headings and subheadings, key talking points and A/B testing ideas for headlines, call to action (CTA) buttons and ad copy.

Of course, it can create the content itself, like other content generators such as Jasper AI and Writesonic; however, AI content always needs editing and fact-checking. The earlier versions of text-generation AIs wrote in a simplistic style that made it obvious that the content was AI generated and marketers found that such content failed to engage readers. Things have improved a lot since the early days, but it's not perfect, and even if the material was written perfectly, these tools are known to make obvious mistakes as well as invent statistics. If you want to retain your credibility, don't take their content at face value – always check for accuracy. Also note that these models are only as good as their training data, so for some extremely niche topics, they might not perform well.

The key is to always focus on the user. Google doesn't penalize high-quality AI content that provides value, but despite how much these language models have improved, it's still unlikely that they'll produce content that's good enough to differentiate your brand. When it comes to SEO, if you only optimize for the search engines, you'll get caught out when their algorithms change, but if you focus on the user, you're in a much better position. As I always say, content really needs to entertain or educate and this is where AI is not up to scratch yet. The human touch is needed if you want to add a unique spin or humour for entertainment value, and when it comes to educating, AI generators still tend to produce generic content that lacks the depth your readers are looking for. What's more, it's quite likely that if your competitors use AI, they will end up with the same content on their site (and one thing Google will penalize is duplicate content). Use AI as a starting point and build on it with information that will genuinely help your audience.

Another task ChatGPT excels at is translation. It can quickly translate marketing materials into multiple languages, enabling you to reach a global audience with localized content (which again should be checked for accuracy). It can also review and edit your copy to ensure that it's error-free and maintains a consistent tone and voice, and you can ask it to generate messaging that aligns with brand guidelines and different customer personas.

ChatGPT can be a valuable tool for market research in several ways. For example, it can help design surveys and questionnaires, ensuring they are structured to elicit useful information. It can gather and synthesize information about specific industries, including trends, key players and market dynamics, and help brainstorm new product ideas and marketing strategies. However, its knowledge is based on the data it's been trained on and it may not be updated with the most current market developments, so its insights should be complemented with up-to-date research and professional expertise. As with SEO and content creation, ChatGPT should be used as a starting point for research.

Of course, ChatGPT is not the only conversational AI on the market – Google and Microsoft have introduced their own versions, Google Bard and Bing Chat. Bard uses Google's own AI model, PaLM 2, instead of GPT-4. It also has some catching up to do – it's more of a work in progress, known to generate inaccurate information. With that said, it has a few useful features that ChatGPT does not. First of all, it can access the internet and therefore offers more current information, whereas ChatGPT is limited to the cutoff date of its training data. In addition, Bard integrates with other Google apps, including Gmail, Docs, Sheets and Colab (a tool for running Python code). Bing Chat is also powered by GPT-4 and is connected to the internet. It's actually integrated into the Bing search engine, which allegedly leads to better search results, and in terms of reliability it's said to outperform Bard.

Generative AI plays a pivotal role in transforming digital communication and media production, particularly in text-to-voice, voice-to-text and text-to-video technologies. Each of these areas leverages the capabilities of AI in unique ways. AI-driven text-to-voice technology converts written text into spoken words, a process that involves several steps. First, NLP is used to understand and process the text, interpreting the syntax and semantics to determine how it should be spoken. Next, speech synthesis is used to generate human-like speech and the models are trained on large datasets of spoken language to reproduce natural-sounding voice, intonation and rhythm. The generative aspect is particularly evident in the way these systems can create realistic speech patterns, intonations and emotions that didn't exist in the original text form.

With voice-to-text, AI transforms spoken words into written text. The models analyse the sound waves of speech to identify phonetic elements, then NLP is used to interpret the context and meaning of the spoken words, ensuring that the text output is grammatically and semantically correct. This technology is widely used in voice assistants, dictation software and accessibility tools.

The advent of generative AI triggered the development of image- and video-generation tools, such as Jasper Art by Jasper AI and Synthesia, one of the most popular video generators. Video is the most engaging medium and is a must for any content strategy, especially when targeting Gen Z. Many video-generation tools use text-to-video algorithms, where users simply enter a text description of the content they want and the AI does the rest. The algorithms interpret the text to generate relevant visual elements, like scenes, characters and objects, which involves understanding the narrative and context. Next, these visual elements are animated and synchronized with generated voiceovers or music, creating a cohesive video. Some of these tools can even create lifelike avatars for talking head-style videos. (AI-powered tools not only generate video content; some enhance the visual and audio elements in existing video.)

Social media algorithms are hungry for video content and it can be tough to keep up with such demands, so we're likely to see these tools being used a lot more in the years to come. Another benefit of image and video generation is that the content is copyright free. Instead of searching for appropriate content on stock websites (and not necessarily finding what's needed), marketers can quickly generate high-quality visual content using AI, without having to worry about copyright.

It's important to note that, as with written content, there's no way to know how original it really is, so that's something to be mindful of. At times, you might end up with output that's quite odd or is far from what you wanted, in which case it can sometimes be easier to just film it yourself. Until the technology develops more, AI image and video generation is not going to be appropriate for all brands; some can start using it as it is right now, it just depends how polished the content needs to be in order to maintain the brand's reputation.

These capabilities open up myriad possibilities, but they also pose unique challenges, particularly in the realm of ethics and authenticity. Issues like deep fakes – AI-generated videos that can make it appear as though individuals are saying or doing things they didn't say or do – raise a wealth of concerns about misinformation. Despite these challenges, their potential is significant when it comes to marketing.

Strategy building and decision support

AI provides marketers with many tools that contribute to strategy building and allows us to be more thorough in our research than ever before. AI-driven analytics and data-mining techniques sift through large datasets to reveal consumer preferences, behaviours and sentiments and this information fuels market research efforts, enabling businesses to tailor products, services and messaging to meet consumer needs and preferences. It also helps with clarifying the customer segments making up an audience by uncovering patterns in purchase behaviour, psychographic factors and so on.

These insights enable effective personalization in marketing campaigns, to the extent of hyper-personalization, where AI can help create personalized content, recommendations and experiences for each customer, increasing engagement and conversion rates.

While we're on the subject of personalization, AI takes it to new levels in email marketing. With dynamic content, emails are personalized for individual users in real-time based on factors such as their location or browsing history. Companies selling physical goods may set their emails to update based on inventory levels; if they're out of stock of a certain item, for example, a different item would be recommended to the customer.

Through predictive analytics, AI can anticipate future market trends and consumer behaviours by analysing historical and real-time data (such as weather forecasts), ensuring businesses are always poised to optimize product offerings at a moment's notice.

The most effective way to leverage customer data is through a customer data platform (CDP). A CDP is a sophisticated tool that aggregates and organizes data across a wide range of touchpoints to create a single, comprehensive customer profile. CDPs aggregate data from multiple sources, such as website visits, social media engagements, email interactions, transactional data, customer service interactions and, increasingly, data gathered from chatbots. The CDP then integrates the data, providing marketers with a coherent and consolidated view of each customer.

A CDP also plays a crucial role in enabling effective omnichannel strategies. The unified view of each customer enables personalization at scale and facilitates accurate segmentation so that marketers can create tailored messages that resonate with each segment, across different channels. CDPs are also helpful for cross-channel attribution, i.e. attributing outcomes to specific channels and interactions, providing insights into which channels are most effective and how they work together to drive customer action. Marketers can then optimize each stage of the customer journey, ensuring they each receive relevant and timely interactions that guide them towards conversion. Finally, using AI-powered analytics on the holistic datasets stored within CDPs enables deep insights that would not be possible by analysing customer data on separate platforms.

Sentiment analysis is another application of AI in marketing. Sentiment analysis uses machine learning and natural language processing to understand and interpret human emotions from text, which serves a few purposes. It can be used to analyse vast amounts of customer feedback, such as reviews, survey responses and social media comments, in order to gauge public sentiment towards a product, brand or service, helping companies understand what customers appreciate and which areas need improvement. Of course, it would be impractical for humans to manually analyse such volumes of textual data, so once again AI provides scalability and thoroughness. Some companies use sentiment analysis specifically for brand monitoring, where the software checks for mentions and discussions about the brand, allowing companies to quickly identify and respond to potential PR crises or capitalize on positive sentiment trends.

Sentiment analysis also helps with market research. AI tools can comb through social media platforms and other sources to analyse trends, opinions and feedback about specific topics, campaigns or products. This provides insights into consumer preferences, helping inform product development and competitive positioning.

AI for SEO and advertising

SEO is one of the cornerstones of digital marketing, but Web 3.0 is set to significantly disrupt the way it works – something I'll discuss in detail in Chapter 14. People are turning to ChatGPT to search for information and in time this may diminish the role of search engines. For now, SEO remains a vital element of any digital marketing strategy and AI is here to make it easier for us.

AI-driven tools analyse search engine algorithms, website content and competitors' strategies to provide actionable recommendations for optimizing web pages. There are many AI SEO tools on the market, one of the most popular being Surfer SEO. It does everything from finding appropriate keywords to generating optimized content to suggesting new content topics. Based on your target keyword, Surfer analyses the keywords on other high-ranking pages on the same topic, then suggests various keywords to include in your content. Essentially, it models your content based on what's already working for your competitors.

You can use its keyword research features and content editor to optimize existing content, or it can generate long-form content for you based on keyword research. Surfer also creates content that's designed to satisfy search intent, making it even more relevant for your audience. In terms of content planning, it analyses social media, forums, news sources and more to find trending topics.

So, AI can improve on-page SEO – but of course, that's not all it takes to rank well. Thankfully, there are tools (such as Semrush) that can analyse off-page SEO through backlink analysis and site auditing, for example.

All these tools not only save time, they also make it easier to rank well even if you don't have much experience with SEO. It's not easy to keep up with the ever-changing search engine algorithms (at least not for humans); with AI, however, there's no need to get bogged down in the finer details as the software quickly adapts.

Now, what about advertising? A lot of work is required to pull off an advertising campaign successfully, from designing ad copy to A/B testing to tracking performance. AI tools, such as BrightBid, automate ad optimization and bidding, saving so much time. Testing has always been essential in marketing and we should be testing as much as possible, but there's only so much that humans can do manually. A machine can run thousands of tests within the same time it would take a human to set up and run three or four. It can test many variations, giving marketers the configuration that is most likely to bring results. BrightBid, for example, constantly adjusts bids, target groups and ad copy, so not only do marketers get to start off with the best-performing ad campaigns, they're also being continually refined for ongoing performance. Tools like this help to level the playing field for smaller teams that otherwise wouldn't have the resources to be so thorough.

AI as a collaborative partner

Digital marketers have always looked to automate jobs that are more suited to machines than humans, but whenever new technologies that automate processes are introduced, there's always the fear that human jobs will be replaced. However, just like with every other technological revolution, AI will augment human capabilities and not replace us. The output of AI models is only as good as the input – so humans need to learn to manage AI and give it the right prompts.

Essentially, AI is akin to having a trusted colleague who excels at handling repetitive tasks and analysing large datasets in a matter of seconds; who prompts us with suggestions we might not have thought of; and who helps fill in the gaps yet lacks the creativity, empathy and strategic vision that humans bring to the table. As such, AI liberates marketing professionals to focus on what they do best: crafting compelling narratives, devising creative campaigns and building authentic connections with their audiences. Humans will guide AI and spend their time focused on big-picture decisions and questions such as: Which consumers do we want to attract? How will we make our money? What products and services do we want to sell?

Marketing jobs are starting to change as a result of AI. Instead of content creators, we may see more content curators and editors, working with AI content to perfect it. Instead of having proofreaders check content written by humans, tools like ChatGPT may be used to check for errors. Also, the traditional role of the data analyst is shifting as software becomes more advanced. Instead of having a dedicated analyst on the team, various marketing roles now include more responsibilities around interpreting insights from AI-powered analytics. That's not to say that the data analyst role will become obsolete, but like anything else, its description may change significantly and, as mentioned, SEO as we know it may change considerably in the years to come. Another emerging role is the creative automation strategist, which involves exploring the best ways to use AI to create marketing assets while maintaining consistent branding. There will also be many more IoT marketing positions in the near future.

Conclusion

If you haven't experimented with any AI tools, now's the time to do it. AI is critical to understand as a core skill set in any job but few more so than marketing. There are AI tools launching daily and there is a strong chance that whatever your role, focus, strategy or issue, there is an AI tool that is at least trying to solve it. If there isn't, perhaps you should build it.

Notes

Perez, S (2023a) OpenAI's ChatGPT app tops 500k downloads in just 6 days. Techcrunch. 25 May, https://techcrunch.com/2023/05/25/chatgpts-new-app-comes-out-of-the-gate-hot-tops-half-a-million-installs-in-first-6-days/ (archived at https://perma.cc/3LPP-MY8P)

Perez, S (2023b) On ChatGPT's first anniversary, its mobile apps have topped 110m installs and nearly $30m in revenue. Techcrunch. 30 November, https://techcrunch.com/2023/11/30/on-chatgpts-first-anniversary-its-mobile-apps-have-topped-110m-installs-and-nearly-30m-in-revenue/ (archived at https://perma.cc/T8F7-584S)

Duarte, F (2024) Number of ChatGPT users. Exploding Topics. 1 March, https://explodingtopics.com/blog/chatgpt-users (archived at https://perma.cc/8CJJ-XE5R)

10

Marketing via the Internet of Things

The Internet of Things is the network of interconnected devices capable of collecting and exchanging data. As of 2023, there were 15.14 billion IoT devices worldwide and this figure is expected to reach 29.42 billion by 2030 (Statista, 2024).

This expansive web of devices, including sensors, smartphones, wearables and smart home appliances, extends internet connectivity beyond the obvious, giving everyday objects advanced functionality. These devices communicate with each other and with centralized systems, which enables them to send and receive data autonomously.

At its core, IoT is about creating a more deeply interconnected world in which the physical and digital realms merge, leading to efficiencies and insights that previously were unattainable. This technology has rapidly become a transformative force across numerous sectors, including healthcare, manufacturing, retail, agriculture and of course marketing.

IoT opens new avenues for marketers to understand and interact with consumers, offering real-time insights that drive personalized and contextually relevant marketing strategies. From smart home devices to wearables, each device becomes a potential touch point for engaging with consumers, allowing brands to seamlessly integrate their messaging into their daily lives. Throughout this chapter we'll review different applications and case studies of IoT in marketing, illustrating its versatility.

FIGURE 10.1 Growth of IoT devices (in billions) 2010–2025

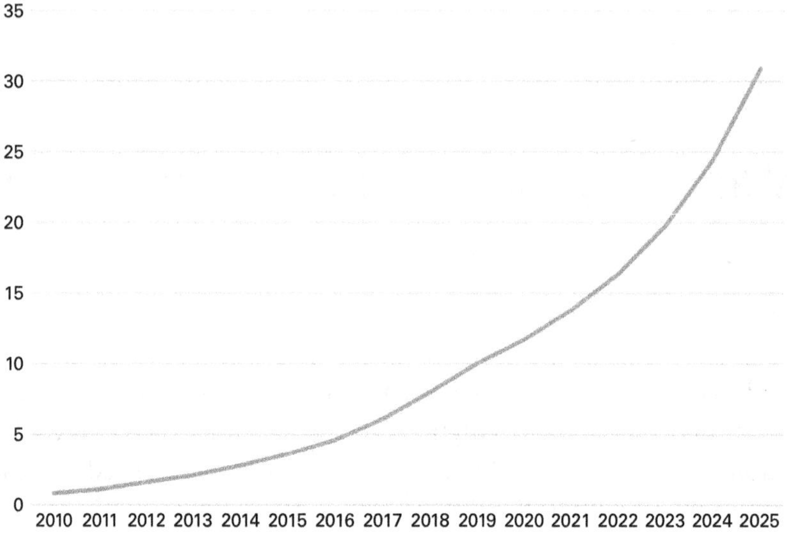

SOURCE Adapted from Howarth, 2023

Smart speakers, voice assistants and home appliances

Sales of smart speakers and voice assistants have exploded in recent years. It's forecast that by 2024, the number of digital voice assistants in use worldwide will have doubled, reaching 8.4 billion (more than the world's current population), compared with the 2020 total of 4.2 billion (Laricchia, 2024).

Products like Amazon Echo and Apple HomePod have become household staples, fundamentally changing how consumers search for information, shop and interact with digital content. This change is largely driven by the convenience and efficiency these devices offer, enabling hands-free operation and personalized, immediate responses. Brands are now leveraging the opportunity, producing audio ad campaigns combined with interactive elements.

CASE STUDY

Purina and Amazon

In 2021, Purina's Beggin' brand collaborated with Amazon on a campaign to raise brand awareness. This creative campaign sought to inspire pet owners to share fun moments with their dogs by introducing the 'Beggin' Boogie', a disco track that users would listen to through Alexa-enabled devices. Pet owners far and wide asked Alexa to 'play the "Beggin' Boogie"' and recorded clips of themselves and their dogs dancing to the music. The campaign was complemented by a series of audio ads.

Daniel McGillivray, Purina's Assistant Brand Manager for Treats Marketing, highlighted the campaign's success in creating special moments for dogs and their owners, leading to impressive engagement rates and cost-per-click efficiencies, as well as bringing in new customers. The 'Beggin' Boogie' took social media by storm, particularly on TikTok and Instagram. The campaign's integration into daily routines, with Alexa playing a central role, was key to its success (Amazon, 2021).

This wasn't the only campaign Purina launched that made use of Alexa. It also created the 'Ask Purina' campaign where new and aspiring dog owners could ask Alexa questions about various breeds, helping them quickly find answers (much faster than searching on Google). Users could learn about different breeds by searching based on different attributes, such as size, energy levels, shedding or non-shedding, helping them get a clearer idea about what breed would be most suitable as a pet (Mobiquity, 2024).

Amazon's IoT services don't stop at smart speakers. It has introduced Amazon Key, a service that lets delivery drivers leave packages inside customers' homes instead of on the doorstep, thus preventing theft. Customers need to have one of Amazon's Cloud Cam home security cameras installed as well as a smart lock and they use the Amazon Key app to get set up. When the driver arrives, they request entry using their scanner and Amazon verifies that the package is designated to the address they're at. The camera then switches on and the door unlocks so the package can be placed inside. While many people may be uncomfortable with someone having access to their home, the security camera lets them watch the delivery being carried out and that's enough for many people to be OK with the arrangement. More recently, Amazon launched In-Garage Delivery – the same process, except customers use smart locks on their garage doors.

Another example is a smart fridge that tracks consumption patterns and notifies users when they're running low on products. It can also reduce energy consumption by alerting users if the door is left open and some models let users adjust the temperature of different compartments in case items have different requirements for preservation. Smart fridges also prevent wastage – users can log items along with their expiry dates and be notified when they're about to spoil so they can use them in time.

IoT's impact on consumer insights

The integration of IoT into marketing has revolutionized the way customer data is collected. Traditional methods often relied on customer surveys or purchase history, but IoT enables the gathering of more granular data from more touchpoints, allowing for a level of personalization and targeting that previously was unattainable.

IoT devices give a continuous stream of real-time data. This not only provides a deep understanding of customer needs and wants, it also allows companies to adapt in real-time and capitalize on opportunities with agility. As a result, they can make quick, informed decisions and tailor their strategies to actual consumer behaviours as they happen. For example, by using IoT to track supply levels and consumer demand in real-time, companies can adopt dynamic pricing models.

The value of real-time data is seen in smart retail systems that track how customers interact with products in-store, providing insights into shopping behaviours, preferences and even the effectiveness of store layouts. Smart shelves are another example, helping optimize stock levels on the shop floor and in warehouses. When low stock levels are detected on the shop floor, staff can be alerted so they can restock, ensuring customers can always find what they need and optimizing revenues. This method is being applied in warehouses, with low inventory levels prompting automatic reordering.

Perhaps one of the best sources of data is wearable technologies, which help businesses understand the intricacies of product use, such as the frequency of use and length of sessions. Prior to IoT, businesses had no way to gather such information when it came to the use of physical products, but now they can gain comprehensive insights into usage habits. This lets them offer timely upgrades or complementary products in a personalized way. IoT devices can also collect data that helps companies detect and fix problems before they become major issues, improving the customer experience.

The data generated by IoT devices can be used to predict consumer behaviours and trends, enabling businesses to proactively market products and services. For instance, by analysing smart home data, a company can predict when a customer might need a replacement for a home appliance and send them an offer before the customer even realizes the need. Another example is using sensors to monitor the number of people entering and exiting a store or venue – based on historical data, staffing requirements can be forecast.

Location-based marketing

IoT enables precise location-based marketing strategies. Using GPS and RFID technologies, businesses can send targeted advertisements and offers to consumers based on their real-time location. There is also beacon technology, where small wireless devices use Bluetooth Low Energy (BLE) to transmit signals to nearby smart devices, typically phones or tablets. It's commonly used in retail, museums, airports and event spaces to provide location-based information, navigation assistance, targeted advertising and interaction opportunities. For example, a retail store can use beacon technology to send special offers to customers' smartphones when they are nearby or in the store, potentially increasing sales. Likewise, a restaurant could send special lunch offers to individuals in nearby office buildings during lunch hours, enhancing the likelihood of attracting customers. Weather data takes things a step further – current conditions and forecasts can be leveraged, increasing the relevance of offers.

Smart billboards are another form of location-based advertising using IoT technology. These billboards collect mobile data from passing devices (for example, GPS data showing that the individual visited Burger King). It then aggregates that data, inferring likely preferences based on the preferences of other users that have visited Burger King. Essentially, it uses a probabilistic model to assess the likely choices of users based on shared behaviour patterns. Based on its conclusions, it can display the right ads at the right time – those that are most likely to convert the people nearby in any given moment. A platform called RADAR by Clear Channel Outdoor Americas (CCOA) was launched in 11 cities that does what I just described. Also note that these applications don't collect personal data (Pymnts, 2016).

Another, simpler example is the use of sensors in venues to monitor foot traffic and adjust the placement ads in real-time to maximize exposure.

Creating unique customer experiences

IoT not only improves the overall customer experience, it can create memorable experiences that differentiate brands. For example, hotels are now using smart room technology – the guest's smartphone becomes a remote control for lighting, heating and other IoT-enabled appliances in the room. Then there are smart fitting rooms for retail, which bring many benefits for customers and businesses alike. Sensors can identify the items a customer brings into the fitting room, then connected screens and mirrors display information on complementary items, colour variations and sizes that are in stock in that specific store, in other stores or online. They can also request for staff to bring items – much more convenient than getting dressed, looking for the items, queueing up again and starting over. Retailers also get to up-sell, cross-sell and gather more data.

The example above shows how IoT helps create omnichannel experiences, where offline and online marketing channels are interconnected. IoT devices will bridge the gap between physical and digital worlds, providing a cohesive experience across various touchpoints and offering more detailed and accurate customer journey mapping.

Now for an example involving wearables. Nivea's IoT print ad in Rio de Janeiro enhanced the experience of families visiting the beach and demonstrated care for the company's customers. Together with the launch of a new sunscreen product for children, the company printed an ad containing a GPS-enabled bracelet. On the beach, children could wear the bracelet and their caregivers would be notified if they moved beyond a safe distance.

Customer experiences at events are also improving thanks to beacon technology. Consider a large exhibition, for example – wearables can gather data on where each user has spent time so they may be notified about similar, upcoming sessions or other relevant exhibitors. They also improve navigation through large venues, giving tips on the best routes to different areas.

Companies are combining IoT with gamification to create engaging experiences. A classic example is Fitbit. When users get started with the app, they're prompted to connect to Facebook and engage with friends that are also using Fitbit, enabling users to share progress and set up challenges. The social element makes it all the more powerful and is key to making such campaigns go viral.

Aside from the direct benefits that IoT brings customers, the operational improvements it creates behind the scenes improve their experiences as well. Again, IoT in retail is promising in this way, as optimized layouts could help optimize foot traffic and prevent crowds. Electronic shelf labels provide up-to-date pricing information – not only does this save retailers the huge amounts of time they spend updating labels manually, it also helps manage customer expectations and eliminate the frustration of going to pay for an item only to discover its actual price is not as displayed. Likewise, in manufacturing, improved processes ensure minimal downtime, optimal productivity and therefore that products are available for customers when they need them.

Challenges and considerations

IoT raises a lot of concerns about security and privacy. Many devices lack robust built-in security features, making them susceptible to hacking and unauthorized access. Devices like smart thermostats and home assistants can be exploited as entry points to access broader home or office networks. A major issue is the fact that devices don't always receive regular updates or patches, including firmware updates, leaving known vulnerabilities unaddressed. In addition, users don't typically change the default passwords for their devices, making it easier for hackers to gain access.

Standardization

The IoT ecosystem lacks standardized security protocols and practices, leading to inconsistencies in security implementations across different devices and systems. What's more, some devices have limited processing power, which restricts the level of security that can be implemented, such as advanced encryption methods. Not all experts agree on this matter, however; research has shown that in some use cases, standard encryption protocols work well, while in others, so-called 'lightweight' encryption methods may be sufficient (Newman, 2019). Also, since IoT devices are often physically accessible, they can be tampered with or have their security compromised through direct physical actions.

Botnets

IoT devices can be targeted and used as part of a botnet, which can then be used to launch large-scale cyberattacks such as distributed denial-of-service (DDoS) attacks. A large-scale botnet attack occurred in 2016, taking down some important websites and services, especially in the US and the UK, including government websites. Chinese manufacturer Hangzhou Xiongmai Technology then recalled 4.3 million of its connected cameras due to a security flaw that allowed malware to be installed on them. The devices were not necessarily targeted during the attack and their recall was a precautionary measure (Burgess, 2016).

These vulnerabilities can have dire consequences in some contexts. With so many devices collecting data, it's possible to build a very detailed profile of a person's life, including their movements, habits and even health markers. This data could be used for malicious purposes such as stalking, manipulation or identity theft. Medical applications of the IoT are also cause for concern, as the hacking of IoT-enabled pacemakers or insulin pumps would cause fatalities. These devices have been recalled in the past due to security threats including the placement of malware directly onto pacemakers. In 2021 alone there were more than 1 billion attacks on IoT-enabled devices, illustrating the urgent need to improve security measures (Marton, 2022).

Privacy

There's also the question of consumer consent and data usage. There's a fine line between personalized marketing and invasive surveillance and we just need to consider the smart billboard example to see how the boundaries are blurred. Yes, these billboards don't collect data that can identify individuals, but having an app track your movements around a city could be seen as invasive. (Nobody seems to mind the fact that the apps we use every day store such data – perhaps it simply feels more invasive when we see the effects of it in such obvious ways.)

Companies need to be transparent about their data-collection methods and usage policies to maintain consumer trust and avoid ethical dilemmas. Rather than being invasive, IoT should be used in a way that is natural and helps customers discover brands and products in novel, interactive ways.

Business opportunity

Moving on from the subject of privacy, it's important to consider the practicalities of different IoT applications and whether they will bring return on investment (ROI). IoT offers numerous options for engaging with customers, but it's important to make sure its use actually aligns with overall business goals and creates genuine value – and to not use it simply because it's trending. As well as assessing the ROI, it's important to understand the target market's receptiveness to IoT interactions. In a similar vein, IoT can lead to data overload if we're not careful; the sheer volume of data generated by devices can be overwhelming and not all of it is useful for marketing purposes. Companies need to develop strategies for data management and analysis to extract meaningful insights without getting lost in the noise.

Sustainability

There are concerns over the sustainability of IoT technologies. It's forecast that in 2025, IoT devices will generate 73.1 zettabytes of data (equal to 1 billion terabytes) (Jovanovic, 2024).

Data centres consume huge amounts of energy; aside from servers, cooling equipment is used because of the amount of heat the servers generate, adding to the energy demands. However, more and more data centres are seeking renewable sources to power their operations and there are various applications in which IoT can be used to conserve energy. Each company is responsible for making ethical choices and supporting green data centres.

Conclusion

The IoT makes marketing an ongoing, interactive experience. Brands can engage with consumers in real-time, delivering relevant content and offers at the right moment, enhancing conversion rates and customer experiences and ultimately deepening brand loyalty. The continual advancement of IoT technologies will introduce new devices such as more sophisticated sensors, improved data-processing techniques and innovative ways to integrate physical and digital experiences, while advancements in AI and machine learning will enable more sophisticated data analysis. In future, this technology will become more cost-effective and therefore more accessible. As such, more and more companies will begin using it in their campaigns. I encourage you to start exploring it now if you have the means.

Notes

Amazon (2021) Inside Purina's strategy to use audio ads and branded experiences with Alexa to play customers the 'Beggin' Boogie'. https://advertising.amazon.com/en-gb/library/case-studies/purina-audio-ads-alexa-skill (archived at https://perma.cc/HL8R-2R4K)

Burgess, M (2016) Chinese IoT firm recalls 4.3 million connected cameras after giant botnet attack. Wired. 25 October, www.wired.co.uk/article/internet-down-dyn-october-2016 (archived at https://perma.cc/7NVF-ZYP6)

Howarth, J (2023) 80+ Amazing IoT statistics (2024–2030). Exploding Topics. 3 November, https://explodingtopics.com/blog/iot-stats (archived at https://perma.cc/LSZ7-8H3C)

Jovanovic, B (2024) Internet of Things statistics for 2024 – taking things apart. DataProt. 6 February, https://dataprot.net/statistics/iot-statistics/ (archived at https://perma.cc/M7DP-X76T)

Laricchia, F (2024) Number of digital voice assistants in use worldwide from 2019 to 2024 (in billions)*. Statista. 14 March, www.statista.com/statistics/973815/worldwide-digital-voice-assistant-in-use/ (archived at https://perma.cc/9STY-KUCW)

Marton, A (2022) SAM: More than 1 billion IoT attacks in 2021. IoTAC. 4 May, https://iotac.eu/sam-more-than-1-billion-iot-attacks-in-2021/ (archived at https://perma.cc/7LT6-JDX2)

Mobiquity (2024) Purina seeks to educate aspiring dog owners. www.mobiquity.com/our-work/ask-purina-alexa-skill-for-dog-lovers (archived at https://perma.cc/72C7-LURE)

Newman, L H (2019) The debate over how to encrypt the Internet of Things. Wired. November 23, www.wired.com/story/lightweight-encryption-internet-of-things/ (archived at https://perma.cc/3SDA-R9UU)

Pymnts (2016) How a smart billboard is changing how consumers interact with products. 23 December, www.pymnts.com/internet-of-things/2016/smart-billboard-advertising/ (archived at https://perma.cc/627M-F2VS)

Statista (2024) Number of Internet of Things (IoT) connected devices worldwide from 2019 to 2023, with forecasts from 2022 to 2030. July, www.statista.com/statistics/1183457/iot-connected-devices-worldwide/ (archived at https://perma.cc/9MUS-KFXP)

11

How marketers have used gamification

In Chapter 5 I explained the importance of gaming in Web3 and why marketers should familiarize themselves with game dynamics. As I said, a much broader demographic plays games now compared with the turn of the century and marketers need to be ready to respond. There is even data showing that 60 per cent of consumers are more likely to buy from a brand if they've enjoyed playing a game it created (Simms, 2019).

As such, it's no surprise that the global gamification market is forecast to be worth $116.68 billion by 2032 (a huge leap from its 2022 value of $10 billion) and many companies are reaping the benefits already (Precedence Research, 2023).

CASE STUDY
Volkswagen

Back in 2012, Volkswagen China adopted gamification principles in a campaign that used crowdsourcing as a way to find ideas for its product line. Users visited the company's website to submit ideas and several winners were selected. VW gained insights into what its target market wanted thanks to the 120,000 submissions and the campaign generated 33 million website visits, maintaining brand awareness (Krows Digital, n.d.).

Target

Likewise, Target developed an app for creating Christmas wish lists which included gamified elements. It generated 75,000 downloads and 100,000 wish lists, equating to potential sales of $92.3 million. In addition, 9,200 new user accounts were set up (Digital Training Academy, n.d.).

Many hotels and online travel agents add game elements to their loyalty programmes. Customers may be rewarded for visiting a certain number of properties, staying at a particular hotel for a certain number of days or booking a certain number of stays. They may also unlock further benefits after reaching spending milestones.

Marketers have always tried to incentivize customers to complete actions and engage with brands and gamification is a powerful way to do it. It doesn't stop at engagement though – the benefits may be more long term. Research has shown that the following so-called dimensions are associated with both cognitive and emotional brand engagement: challenge, feedback, autonomy, immersion and interaction. In turn, these forms of engagement motivate further usage intention. This highlights the potential of gaming since it involves all five dimensions (Jung et al., 2021). With that in mind, this chapter will cover some important gaming concepts that you can integrate into your marketing strategies, along with some case studies of successful campaigns.

Gamification concepts

Gamification takes many forms in marketing, from simple rewards schemes to comprehensive experiences that are clearly recognizable as games. Gamification involves applying the psychological principles used in games in a non-game context, which for our purposes is marketing. Games play on a few fundamental, instinctive motivations that humans have, such as the tendency towards goal-oriented behaviour, to compete, to receive rewards and to feel the satisfaction of achieving goals. They also tap into the need for social connection.

The Octalysis Framework by gamification expert Yu-Kai Chou refers to eight drivers of human behaviour that we see in games: epic meaning and calling (such as the call to complete a quest); development and accomplishment; empowerment of creativity and feedback; ownership and possession (i.e. collecting game assets); social influence and relatedness, or envy; scarcity and impatience; unpredictability and curiosity; and loss and avoidance (or the fear of losing something).

Games use various mechanisms in order to fulfil these drives – some simple, some more complex. The most accessible and easy-to-implement game elements include checklists and progress bars. In such cases, the simple actions the user completes are intrinsically rewarding; the user is presented with a trigger (i.e. a list to be checked off) and this opens a reward loop which they feel compelled to close by completing the action/s. Articles that contain progress bars as users scroll down the page are another simple example that keep users engaged in the content. Likewise, LinkedIn uses progress bars to encourage users to complete their profiles. Note that there's nothing for users to win here – yet they're still driven to act based on these fundamental human tendencies. In fact, the only one that wins is LinkedIn by collecting data.

Points are a fundamental measure of progress or achievement, motivating users to continue engaging with a task or system. They serve a similar purpose as rewards, yet rewards are also used to incentivize specific behaviours (as well as overall engagement). Collecting points is also a way for users to win rewards and we see this in many loyalty programmes where points are awarded for purchases or engagement, their accumulation leading to discounts or other benefits. Some experiences involve challenges and quests that users have to complete in order to win points and progress to new levels. For example, a restaurant might challenge customers to try all menu items within a month to win a prize (this strategy also uses the principles of scarcity and urgency to motivate immediate action).

A good example of a points-based loyalty programme is that of Starbucks. The programme is multi-tiered, with customers unlocking a new level of rewards after earning points. They can win extra points and offers by paying for their purchases using the Starbucks Rewards Visa Card in various stores, enabling them to earn points on non-Starbucks purchases. They can also play games to earn points, such as the famous 'Starbucks for Life' programme as well as 'Star Days', where customers win rewards by playing arcade games.

Leaderboards rank users based on their performance or achievements, tapping into the competitive spirit and encouraging users to improve their position relative to others. Badges and titles perform a similar function, not only demonstrating accomplishment but motivating continued participation in order to reach higher positions. They also tap into the desire for recognition and status. Brands use them all the time. One example is Booking.com, which uses different titles within its loyalty scheme depending on how much a customer has spent on the platform. Similar mechanisms are seen in fitness apps that award people for achieving milestones. Brands encourage users to share these achievements through social media, adding to the positive reinforcement as their audience provides validation. Badges are common in communities surrounding a brand, demonstrating their level of contribution to the community.

Levels indicate a user's stage of progress in a gamified system and advancing to higher levels typically unlocks new challenges or rewards. Retail apps often incorporate levels to indicate a customer's loyalty status, higher levels unlocking exclusive benefits or offers. This approach taps into our curiosity and the desire to see what the next level holds. Also, having immediate feedback keeps players on track towards their goals and again, the likes of progress bars achieve this objective.

Some gamified marketing campaigns are built around a narrative or story in which customers play a key role. This could be a journey where each purchase or engagement represents a step in the story, for example. Storytelling is something primal and universal – something everyone can get on board with. As such, it makes the brand interaction more memorable and engaging. A narrative also provides context and meaning to tasks, making them more interesting and enjoyable.

Allowing users to customize aspects of their experience, such as creating avatars or user profiles, can increase emotional investment while integrating social elements (such as sharing achievements or competing with friends) leverages social motivation. Another way that brands incorporate the social aspect is through referral schemes, rewarding both parties for participation in the shared experience.

Nike's Run Club app is a great example of how the social aspect of gamification drives engagement. Users can set up and monitor their personalized training regime and compete in challenges, winning badges and trophies. They can also create and participate in community challenges with friends and family. The app tracks metrics and provides training tips; combined with invoking community spirit and competition, this provides genuine value and keeps customers returning to the brand.

For a gamified experience to be successful, it needs to be designed with some key psychological triggers in mind. There's a whole science behind this (behaviour science), but a few points to remember include rewards (positive and negative reinforcement), instant gratification, social pressure and the fear of missing out.

Various studies have proven that negative reinforcement can be just as effective – and sometimes more so – than positive reinforcement. Negative reinforcement is when an undesirable stimulus is taken away, such as the removal of the number of notifications a user has on an app icon. Users feel compelled to click on the icon so that the number will no longer be displayed; once the app is open, they start using it, even if they didn't intend to before.

Players may be driven to pursue the long-term goals a game sets out but it's important to give them instant gratification as well. They want to get a hit of dopamine as soon as possible instead of having to play for hours and that's why games contain small rewards along the journey, such as winning points when users collect certain objects. For longer, more involved game experiences, this is important. In terms of social pressure, the drive to not let down other team members is a powerful motivator, while FOMO (fear of missing out) can be leveraged in many ways (limited-time offers, exclusive items or content, etc.).

While we're on the topic of rewards, it's important to mention intrinsic vs extrinsic motivation. Extrinsic motivation is where actions are driven by external rewards or pressures, while intrinsic motivation refers to the drive to engage in an activity for its inherent satisfaction. Both types of rewards are important.

Gamification taps into intrinsic motivation by making the experience inherently enjoyable or satisfying. This could be through the challenge, the joy of mastering a skill, the excitement of competition or the pleasure of achieving a personal best. To put it into perspective, consider a fitness app that gamifies the experience of exercising. Badges or points can motivate users, but the intrinsic motivation comes with the satisfaction of completing a tough workout or the pleasure of improving one's health. When users are intrinsically motivated, they have a good basis for engaging with the product or platform consistently and over a longer period, leading to higher user retention.

Finally, I'll touch on communities. Communities are central to Web3 and gamification has a big part to play in creating them. UGC has always strengthened communities surrounding a brand and combining them with gamification is a potent mix (we only have to think about the success of TikTok's branded hashtag challenges to realize that). Gamification encourages users to create content that aligns with brand values and by rewarding contributions, brands further the sense of community and belonging, while also benefiting from authentic and original content. The power of gamification in communities is also seen on platforms where users earn points for contributing ideas, participating in discussions or helping other community members.

The convergence of gamification and Web3 technologies

Web3 technologies provide a more interactive, immersive and personalized internet experience, characteristics that naturally complement gamification. Do you remember the example from Chapter 4 about how Burger King Russia used cryptocurrency to reward customers in its Whoppercoin campaign? Well, it wasn't the only fast-food joint to get in on the action. American fast-food chain Shake Shack also introduced a promotion where customers were rewarded for purchases with Bitcoin (15 per cent of the value of every purchase was paid back in Bitcoin) (Edge, 2022).

It's not just retail where crypto rewards schemes are taking off. In 2022, American Express announced its first crypto rewards credit card, rewarding users with crypto for any purchases, among other perks (Bambysheva, 2022).

Crypto isn't the only way to incentivize customers using blockchain technology. Tokens can be incorporated into loyalty programmes, where customers earn tokens for purchases, social media engagement or participating in brand challenges. These tokens can then be redeemed for discounts, exclusive products or unique brand experiences, adding tangible value to consumer interactions with the brand. NFTs can be used as one-of-a-kind rewards for consumer participation, offering collectability and exclusivity (i.e. FOMO), which can significantly increase the motivation to participate.

Of course, smart contracts enable customers to be rewarded automatically once they've completed certain actions or achieved specific milestones. For instance, a customer might complete a series of brand-engagement activities, such as sharing content on social media, reviewing products or participating in surveys. Upon completion, a smart contract could automatically release rewards.

This highlights an interesting trend: customers are increasingly being rewarded simply for engaging with marketing content. Another example of this is the 'Watch-to-Earn' model, where consumers are rewarded for watching ads.

Speaking of advertising, advergaming is a tactic we'll be seeing much more of in Web3. With advergaming, games are used as a medium to promote a brand, product or message. It can be subtle, like branded items or logos within the game environment, or more direct, where the entire game is built around the brand's theme or products. 'The Great Bucket Hunt' by KFC is an example of the latter. This AR game was KFC's answer to *Pokémon GO*, but instead of hunting Pokémon, users had to find virtual Buckets located around the country. Each bucket came with a prize, including free food, sports experiences and cash of up to $50,000.

How else are companies combining VR and AR technologies with gamification? Another successful campaign was that by watch brand Seiko, which created a VR tennis challenge in the lead-up to the 2019 Australian Open. The campaign was set up in Melbourne's Federation square, lasted two days and had 400 participants. Using a physical VR tennis racket, participants stood opposite a virtual version of brand ambassador and world champion Novak Djokovic, on a Seiko-branded virtual court. They had to return his serve and hit targets to win points. The winner received $1,000 and a Novak Djokovic special-edition watch (Initiative (NSW), 2019).

How are brands including these types of experiences within the metaverse? Of course, not every brand is going to create its own world like Nikeland, so what are the other options? Businesses are looking to solutions such as gamified ads within existing metaverse worlds, as well as virtual billboards, shopfronts and other assets. I'll be discussing this topic in detail in the next chapter.

What about the Internet of Things? As the IoT continues to grow, we're seeing it being integrated into loyalty schemes and again, Starbucks is a leading example. The company has installed beacons in some stores which send customers messages about promotions and information on premium blends as a way to up-sell.

Key considerations for designing gamified experiences

To start creating gamified experiences, businesses must first define the objectives of the campaign, as this informs the behaviours that customers need to take. For example, if building a community is necessary for success, interaction among members needs to be incentivized; if it is simply a case of increasing sales, then purchases and actions earlier in the funnel need to be incentivized.

It's also important to consider the target market and what type of gamification they will respond well to – for example, gamification will not always be appropriate in B2B interactions, but it can be. (A case study where it was successful was in 2017 when Honda teamed up with Aesthetic Group to create an experience that would increase dealership buy-in of its new Civic Hatch. The campaign was designed to educate staff on the new model and included video content and gamification elements such as competitions and virtual treasure hunts.)

People make a number of common mistakes when creating a gamified experience. One is focusing too much on the gameplay and not enough on moving the customer towards the business goal, i.e. generating leads, sales and so on. Thorough planning and design should prevent this. It's also important to balance challenge and skill; experiences should be challenging enough to engage in but not so difficult that it becomes frustrating. Also avoid overly complex rules that might deter engagement.

It's essential to offer customers the right rewards – ones that are genuinely valuable. Using tools such as badges and leaderboards will drive engagement, but if the actual rewards aren't worth it, that engagement won't last. Always test the user response to ensure gamification elements and rewards are effective and adjust the strategy until a successful formula is found. Make sure the value proposition of the game is clearly communicated to your audience – the last thing you want is to mislead them and create disappointment.

Once again, incorporate social elements where possible and focus on storytelling. So many successful games have a powerful narrative and that's no coincidence. Make sure the story is relevant to the brand and resonates with your target audience.

It's also important to consider the different types of players and how you can satisfy their motivations. Game researcher Richard A Bartle defined four player types based on common characteristics: Achievers, Explorers, Socializers and Killers. Achievers are very goal-driven, so winning points, progressing through levels and showing off their status will appeal to them. Meanwhile Explorers are drawn to discovering new areas within a game and are less concerned about outcomes. Socializers are more into collaborating with other players and the extent to which they're goal-focused will vary. Finally, Killers are the least common type of player. They're similar to Achievers in that they're goal-focused, except seeing others lose while they win is important to them. The way each type of player relates to narrative will vary as well – for example, the Achiever may be consumed by the epic objective they need to attain while the Explorer may be more drawn to the setting.

I'm not saying all gamified experiences must satisfy all types of users in every way possible, but it's important to recognize how varied your audience is. For more comprehensive gaming experiences, it is important to design for different types of players.

Conclusion

Hopefully this chapter has given you some inspiration for creating gamified experiences – from the simple use of progress bars to crypto rewards to full-on VR games. Like I said, you may not be a fan of gaming, but it looks like it's here to stay, so it's wise to start implementing gamification in your campaigns. There are always opportunities to gamify customers' interactions with your brand, so keep a lookout for them.

Notes

Bambysheva, N (2022) American Express announces first crypto rewards credit card on its network. Forbes. 10 June, www.forbes.com/sites/ninabambysheva/2022/06/10/american-express-announces-first-crypto-rewards-credit-card-on-its-network/?sh=31d5e69c48d5 (archived at https://perma.cc/T43W-KT8N)

Digital Training Academy (n.d.) Mobile gaming case study: Target becomes Santa's helper with 'Holiday Wish' app. www.digitaltrainingacademy.com/casestudies/2015/11/mobile_gaming_case_study_target_becomes_santas_helper_with_holiday_wish_app.php (archived at https://perma.cc/EXB7-PWBB)

Edge, A (2022) Can crypto rewards win over gen-Z consumers? Raconteur. March, www.raconteur.net/customer-experience/can-crypto-rewards-win-over-gen-z-consumers (archived at https://perma.cc/HDA7-J4G7)

Initiative (NSW) (2019) Seiko and Initiative serve up new VR Australian Open experience. 16 January, www.adnews.com.au/campaigns/seiko-and-initiative-serve-up-new-vr-australian-open-experience (archived at https://perma.cc/U5GA-7Y4N)

Jung, J, Yu, J, Seo, Y and Ko, E (2021) Consumer experiences of virtual reality: Insights from VR luxury brand fashion shows, *Journal of Business Research*, June. https://yonsei.elsevierpure.com/en/publications/consumer-experiences-of-virtual-reality-insights-from-vr-luxury-b (archived at https://perma.cc/2NH7-HWL5)

Krows Digital (n.d.) Gamification: All about increasing interactions and revenues. https://krows-digital.com/gamification-in-digital-marketing-all-about-increasing-interactions-and-revenues/ (archived at https://perma.cc/XFH7-SEVA)

Precedence Research (2023) Gamification market. August, www.precedenceresearch.com/gamification-market (archived at https://perma.cc/3HV8-YTA8)

Simms, B (2019) 5 benefits of using gamification in your digital marketing strategy. Digital Marketing World Forum. 13 May, www.digitalmarketing-conference.com/5-benefits-of-using-gamification-in-your-digital-marketing-strategy/ (archived at https://perma.cc/6SG6-C6XH)

12

Learnings from existing
mini metaverses

'Mini metaverse' is a term used to describe the smaller-scale, self-contained virtual worlds or digital environments that share some characteristics with a fully fledged metaverse but are more limited in scope. I've mentioned a few case studies in previous chapters but let's recap on how these worlds, or mini metaverses, work.

Mini metaverses represent a subset of the broader metaverse concept and aim to provide immersive experiences through elements like VR, AR or 3D graphics. Users can often create their own content, such as avatars, objects or structures, and interact with the creations of others. Mini metaverses also facilitate social interactions, allowing users to communicate, collaborate or compete with each other within the virtual space.

Mini metaverses are typically smaller in scale and may focus on specific themes, industries or activities. They may also serve as testing grounds for metaverse-related concepts, allowing users and developers to explore the potential of virtual spaces and interactions. So, while they offer elements of the metaverse experience, they do not encompass the vast interconnected digital universes that are envisioned in discussions of the full metaverse.

Mini metaverses often incorporate their own economic systems, enabling users to buy, sell or trade virtual goods and services, in some cases using virtual currencies or tokens. It may sound bizarre to some that people would spend money on digital assets, but gamers have long been paying for in-game assets, so the idea of paying for others such as virtual land and branded merchandise is not too big a stretch of the imagination. Besides, we don't need to imagine it anymore as many brands, including the NFL, have launched virtual stores selling virtual merch for avatars – and fans are paying.

Again, a virtual world does not have to involve VR to be considered a metaverse. For example, the City of London Corporation partnered with NexTech AR Solutions to create a mini metaverse to help users explore arts and culture in the capital. Users download the 'Harmony at London Wall Place' app to take part in the experience, which lets them view AR works of art and curated visuals and music from the London Symphony Orchestra and the Guildhall School of Music and Drama (Cureton, 2021).

Mini metaverses offer unique opportunities for brands to engage with their audiences, experiment with immersive experiences and lay the groundwork for what could eventually become a fully fledged metaverse. Marketers are using virtual worlds not only to generate new revenue streams but to interact with customers in novel ways that are not possible on existing channels – and to create integrated experiences.

In the future, greater collaboration between platforms may lead to greater interoperability, potentially leading to the concept of one overarching metaverse. However, estimations from Meta itself state this may take another 5–10 years. The crypto community, among others, have criticized the idea, partly because it goes against the principle of decentralization.

In this chapter we will explore some examples of mini metaverses and delve into how brands are actively participating in these spaces.

FIGURE 12.1 Monthly active users of mini metaverses (in millions)

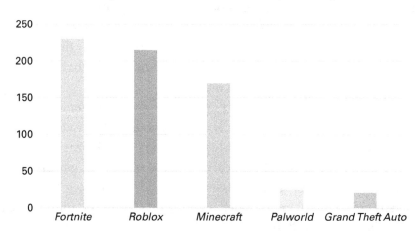

SOURCE Shewale, 2023, 2024; Woodward, 2024; Strickland, 2024; Apolinario, 2024

Minecraft

Minecraft, the iconic sandbox game by Mojang Studios, has captured the hearts and minds of around 100 million users worldwide. Its open-world format allows players to explore, build, interact with each other and trade items in a limitless virtual environment. The platform is owned by Microsoft, yet it's decentralized; nobody controls the game or what players can do within it, anyone can create a metaverse on the platform and each metaverse has its own rules. It also democratizes access since it can run with a very low-tech setup; no expensive VR headsets required. It's therefore a great starting place for anyone wanting to experiment and get a feel for what the metaverse has to offer. Beyond gaming and marketing, people are using it for educational purposes such as simulating ancient civilizations.

Minecraft's rules for marketing are stricter than those of other platforms, but brands are finding ways to leverage it with their permission. For example, Procter & Gamble created a 'P&G World', where customers can attend virtual events, participate in competitions and test virtual products through interactive experiences (such as testing different styles using Gillette razors or washing virtual clothes with Tide detergent). There's also an educational, corporate social responsibility (CSR) element – the company created interactive materials on how it is reducing plastic waste and advice on ecological laundry practices (Metaverse 911, n.d.).

Another notable case study is that of Kellogg's. The brand observed that its audience had given family time more priority since the pandemic and so created an experience that families could partake in together. On the platform, users designed a playground that would end up being built in the real world for a community in need; not only did users spend more quality time together, they were contributing to a good cause at the same time. Kellogg's also offered 350 Minecoins per purchase as an incentive for participation.

The experience was promoted across various channels, including in-store displays, social media and collaborations with influencers. The brand also built a *Minecraft* microsite that encouraged participation.

The campaign generated 379 social media impressions (and that was just on Facebook, Instagram and Pinterest) and sales grew by 11 per cent, combined with $85 million in incremental gross sales volume compared with the year before (May, 2023).

Fortnite

The *Fortnite* metaverse is another platform to watch out for, known for several different gameplay options including the most popular, Battle Royale. This mode supports up to 100 players on an island competing for resources and engaging in battles to be the last one standing (the last player or team). There's also the 'Save the World' mode, centred around the idea of saving the world from a storm. The gameplay involves fighting zombies, building structures and completing various missions. Finally, the 'Creative' mode enables users to build maps, games and challenges.

UGC is a key tenet of the *Fortnite* metaverse, with players designing their own worlds, skins and more, and they can also engage in creative competitions. The *Fortnite* metaverse supports real-time interaction between players and enables cross-platform play – users can participate from various devices, including PC, mobile, Xbox and PlayStation.

The creative freedom *Fortnite* provides has enabled brands to explore unique marketing opportunities. Notably, the partnership with LEGO gave players access to an open-ended gaming experience that blurs the lines between the physical LEGO toy and the digital world. Users can play alone or with friends and each LEGO *Fortnite* world created is unique. Users can do everything from simply creating virtual LEGO structures to exploring the vast environment or going on adventures to tackle enemies. They can also build villages and more expansive worlds. Players interact with different characters and creatures, some of which come from *Fortnite* itself while others are made from LEGO bricks.

Wendy's also developed a *Fortnite* campaign thanks to the launch of the platform's 'Food Fight' mode. Players fought a battle between the two restaurants of the *Fortnite* universe, the so-called Durr Burger and Pizza Pit. Durr Burger was represented as storing its meat in freezers, so Wendy's used this as a way to promote the fact it only uses fresh meat. In concrete terms, it took the side of the opposition and had the objective of smashing freezers with a pick-axe. This was streamed on Twitch and gained more than 1.5 million minutes of watching time. The collaboration gave Wendy's an organic way to reach its audience and communicate its message.

Roblox

Roblox has always been more focused on social interaction compared with *Fortnite* and provides more flexibility in terms of creating open-ended experiences rather than just games. However, with its release of Creative Mode 2.0, *Fortnite* is transitioning away from being just a gaming platform. Both platforms have millions of monthly active users and hold great potential for marketers.

Fashion retailer Vans used *Roblox* to create the online skate park Vans World, which has had more than 48 million visitors since its launch. In Vans World, users buy (and design) virtual items for their avatars. They can win points through gameplay and exchange them for virtual products, explore skate sites and design custom skateboards in a virtual store.

Gucci is another brand at the forefront of metaverse innovation. In one of its experiments designed to attract Gen Z consumers, the luxury fashion brand hosted a two-week virtual art installation on the platform based on its real-life 'Gucci Garden'. The exhibition had a range of themed rooms where users could browse virtual products and buy them for their avatars. Gucci has also created virtual assets for various games, including *Sims, The*. (The market for selling virtual goods for avatars is already worth $54 billion annually. If you're still not convinced, perhaps this will change your mind: Gucci sold a virtual version of its Dionysus bag for $4,115, which is higher than the value of the real-world product (Hazan et al., 2022).)

Of course, McDonald's has got in on the action as well. The fast-food chain worked with DeuSens, a company whose expertise lies in using interactive technologies to optimize marketing processes and enhance its clients' brand image. The campaign targeted McDonald's' Latin American audience, with the goal of expanding the brand's presence in the virtual world and creating experiences that would help it connect with new generations of consumers. The result was McDonald's Land, one of the largest virtual spaces ever created in *Roblox*. It included five islands designed to raise awareness of the four products in the McCombo Pro, a menu created to promote the new virtual experience. Each island had a unique aesthetic and distinct gamification elements. On all the islands, users could collect virtual coins to exchange for wearables and skins that featured design elements characteristic of McDonald's Land (purchased at the virtual world's restaurant). Within a few short weeks of its launch, the campaign had had 300,000 visits and helped the brand position itself as a leader in interactive innovation.

Grand Theft Auto

Grand Theft Auto has always walked the line between standard gameplay and metaverse-like experiences. Even with its focus on narrative and completing missions, players have plenty to explore within the environment (which also has its own currency). Greenpeace actually used the game to raise awareness about climate issues. In partnership with creative agency VMLY&R Brazil, it recreated the virtual city of Los Santos to demonstrate the possible effects of climate change, showing what it would look like with certain areas and landmarks submerged by water.

GTA Online has even more experiential elements than earlier versions of the game and things are likely to progress significantly with the release of *GTA VI*, due to launch in 2025. Rumour has it that this version will be more of a metaverse platform than a traditional game and we're already seeing hints of the direction it could take. For example, *GTA Online* launched an expansion called 'The Contract', part of which involves hanging out with a virtual Dr Dre while he's recording a track. Again, this has nothing to do with the gameplay, it's just an added experience. There is also speculation that *GTA VI* will come with its own in-game cryptocurrency.

GTA is one of the most popular games of all time: more than 200 million units of *GTA V* have been sold since its release in 2013 and *GTA Online* is used by hundreds of thousands of players at any given moment. With that in mind, the release of a *GTA* metaverse could be highly influential in terms of the overall development of the metaverse. For the time being, Rockstar Games don't support VR, but who knows what's in store in the future.

Other mini metaverses

Beyond these major gaming platforms, various other virtual worlds have emerged where users can create characters, construct environments, alter physics and make transactions. Notable examples include *Second Life, VRChat and Decentraland*, which I touched upon before.

A range of businesses is now involved in *Decentraland*. For example, Coca-Cola collaborated with 3D creators at Tafi to create an auction experience. Users would bid to win special-edition virtual loot boxes containing NFTs, including *Decentraland* wearables. The campaign brought in more than $1 million in revenues.

JPMorgan has also taken the leap and created a virtual lounge in *Decentraland*, claiming to be the first major lender to enter the metaverse. The so-called Onyx Lounge is named after the company's Onyx blockchain unit, which offers Ethereum-based services. This move is not surprising: JPMorgan states that the market value of the metaverse could be as high as $1 trillion per annum and that NFTs have a market cap of $1 billion (Paige, 2022; JPMorgan, 2022).

Decentraland is a good platform for companies whose values align with the principles of decentralization, since it's the world's largest decentralized blockchain platform at present.

Meta *Horizon Worlds* is a 3D social platform where users can play games, interact with other users and attend virtual concerts. Originally, it could be accessed through VR only, but that has now changed. *Horizon Worlds* is home to far fewer worlds than the major platforms and its user base is far smaller, but brands are still using it to reach consumers. In fact, Wendy's created a virtual restaurant experience in *Horizon Worlds*, where users could explore products, play mini-games and attend concerts in partnership with iHeartRadio. In addition, users could make real orders for delivery or collection within the virtual world. This illustrates how we can create integrated experiences (the topic of the next chapter).

Key considerations

Marketers need to start planning ahead, assessing the new skills their teams will require and experimenting with the mini-metaverse concept. There's going to be a lot to learn: we're entering uncharted territory, which means that what we've done before may not apply in the metaverse.

The first step when considering any new strategy is to ask yourself, why are we doing this? Your motivation might be the revenue potential in general, or the fact that your competitors are already using the metaverse. These are valid points, of course, but you need to consider why your brand in particular should be in the metaverse and what your goals are. Are you trying to reach a younger audience? Do you

FIGURE 12.2 Searches for 'metaverse' (larger line) and 'metaverse marketing' demonstrate an initial spike and while the volume has understandably dropped since, the search terms remain

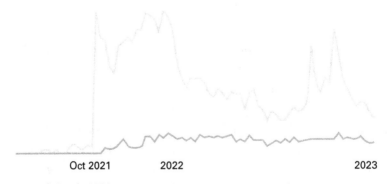

Oct 2021   2022   2023

SOURCE Google Trends, 2024

want to demonstrate that you're an innovative brand? Such questions will guide your resource use and ensure that what you're doing is in the best interests of your audience.

For example, companies are mostly targeting Gen Z and Millennials when using such technologies; you don't want to start alienating the rest of your customer base by investing too much in appealing to these segments. It's just as important to cater to your other customers and maintain their trust. So, businesses need to find the right balance between immersive, metaverse experiences and traditional channels to reach their audience; the metaverse is not an all-or-nothing matter.

Creating native experiences in the metaverse and measuring them through native metrics is crucial for brands looking to establish a meaningful presence in this emerging realm. The metaverse is a unique environment with its own set of rules and user expectations and treating it like any other marketing channel is unlikely to yield the desired results. Users expect to engage with brands in a way that feels integrated into the virtual world, so copying the strategies used on other channels can come across as intrusive and out of place. As such, brands that create native experiences will demonstrate respect for user expectations and will come across as more authentic as a result.

Marketers need to measure their success using appropriate metrics and these won't necessarily be the same ones we use for other channels. Engagement metrics to consider may relate to time spent in the metaverse, the amount of UGC, the number of social interactions unique to the metaverse, data on NFT transactions and so on.

Virtual worlds thrive on community-driven interactions and brands that foster user participation and co-creation may generate more meaningful connections. This is important for long-term relationship building, a vital driver of building a solid presence in the metaverse. Brands may also benefit from holding live events such as virtual product launches; live video streaming is a powerful relationship-building tool in a non-virtual context and the benefits are likely to translate.

Collaboration is essential. We've gone through many case studies in this chapter that involved new strategic partnerships. In addition, influencer marketing will be just as important as it is now.

Conclusion

As I always say, don't wait until it's too late before you start experimenting. Even if you have no immediate plans to create a mini metaverse, there's no harm in tinkering with different platforms and building a picture of how to leverage them in future. Partnering with creators in these spaces is also a really smart way to bring your brand into established mini metaverses. Consider your opportunities here and take the step that best fits your brand journey.

Notes

Apolinario, T (2024) How many people play GTA V in 2024? (User & growth stats). Fiction Horizon, 23 January, https://fictionhorizon.com/how-many-people-play-gta-v-user-growth-stats/ (archived at https://perma.cc/4B9L-NA3N)

Cureton, D (2021) Nextech builds 'mini-metaverse' for City of London. XR Today. 13 October, www.xrtoday.com/augmented-reality/nextech-builds-mini-metaverse-for-city-of-london/ (archived at https://perma.cc/2MCZ-SH5W)

Hazan, E, Kelly, G, Khan, H, Spillecke, D and Yee, L (2022) Marketing in the metaverse: An opportunity for innovation and experimentation. McKinsey. 24 May, www.mckinsey.com/capabilities/growth-marketing-and-sales/our-insights/marketing-in-the-metaverse-an-opportunity-for-innovation-and-experimentation (archived at https://perma.cc/EXE4-QVKN)

JPMorgan (2022) Opportunities in the metaverse. www.jpmorgan.com/content/dam/jpm/treasury-services/documents/opportunities-in-the-metaverse.pdf (archived at https://perma.cc/E8HE-J6ZE)

May, A (2023) A Gaming Partnership Between Kellogg's and Minecraft. Ana.net. May 20, www.ana.net/miccontent/show/id/cs-2023-05-reggie-kelloggs-525311568 (archived at https://perma.cc/L4MB-PFZA)

Metaverse 911 (n.d.) Procter & Gamble World on Minecraft. www.metaverse911.rs/top-30-metaverse-experiences/procter-gamble-world-on-minecraft (archived at https://perma.cc/4KA8-YZX7)

Paige, W (2022) Big banks take plunge into metaverse as JPMorgan enters '$1 trillion industry'. Emarketer. 17 February, www.insiderintelligence.com/content/big-banks-plunge-metaverse-jpmorgan-enters-1-trillion-industry-onyx (archived at https://perma.cc/UKW3-NSYS)

Shewale, R (2023) *Fortnite* statistics for 2024 (active players, revenue & more). Demandsage. 16 December, www.demandsage.com/*fortnite*-statistics/#:~:text= Fortnite%20has%20500%20million%20registered,revenue%20came%20in%20 2022%20alone (archived at https://perma.cc/38ZK-YPKU)

Shewale, R (2024) Roblox statistics for 2024 (active players, revenue & usage). Demandsage. 15 January, www.demandsage.com/how-many-people-play roblox/#:~:text=Creators%20David%20Baszucki%20and%20Eric,216%20 million%20monthly%20active%20users (archived at https://perma.cc/PQY4-FNXL)

Strickland, D (2024) Palworld reached 25 million players in a month. TweakTown, 23 February, www.tweaktown.com/news/96411/palworld-reached-25-million-players-in-month/index.html#:~:text=Palworld%20reached%2025%20 million%20players%20in%20a%20month (archived at https://perma.cc/N6XL-X8NX)

Woodward, M (2024) Minecraft user statistic: How many people play Minecraft in 2024? Search Logistic. 15 February, www.searchlogistics.com/learn/statistics/ minecraft-user-statistics/#:~:text=Minecraft%20has%20over%20166%20 million,revenue%20in%2Dgame%20sales%20alone (archived at https:// perma.cc/4A6V-WEWS)

13

Integrated marketing 2.0

Integrated marketing is a strategic approach that combines various marketing methods and channels to create a unified, cohesive experience for the audience. It's about ensuring that all marketing activities work together in harmony to provide a consistent message and experience; no marketing activity should be conducted in isolation without considering how it fits into the bigger picture. This area is a passion of mine and formed the basis of my best-selling book *Digital Marketing Strategy*. Now, in my mind at least, we are moving into phase two of this important strategic approach. Integrated marketing 2.0 brings brands, channels and consumers all together into one fully immersive place that harnesses all aspects of affective marketing and *must* deliver it simultaneously, consistently and completely.

Without this approach, businesses may give mixed messages or lack a strong brand identity, potentially jeopardizing brand awareness and customer loyalty. Web 3.0 represents a new frontier for integrated marketing, offering boundless opportunities for brands to connect different aspects of their marketing efforts.

Principles of integration

As I mentioned above, my first book, *Digital Marketing Strategy*, includes a chapter dedicated to explaining the principles of integration. I'll briefly go over a few key points now.

As you will know, a multi-channel approach requires using a combination of channels to reach the target audience where they're most likely to engage and this could include a mix of online and offline channels. Naturally, a fundamental pillar of such integrated strategies is consistent brand messaging and customer experience across all channels. A simple example is that a customer should have the same quality of experience when viewing content on a mobile app as with a website. Similarly, a customer using a chatbot should receive the same standard of service as they would when talking to a sales assistant directly, whether in a physical store or through any digital medium.

The core message and tone should remain consistent, with different channels reinforcing each other; the same goes for adhering to visual identity guidelines. However, the more channels a brand uses, the harder it becomes to remain consistent, which is why it's important to develop a strategy to inform this approach and continually review the data to make sure everything is in order. Multi-channel analysis measures the success of integrated marketing, highlighting discrepancies across channels that might need addressing. Of course, determining the ROI of integrated marketing is complex, which is why an analytics solution designed to carry out the task is a worthwhile investment.

Multi-channel analysis not only helps ensure consistency, it also provides insights into the variation in consumer preferences and behaviours across different channels. Understanding these variations allows marketers to tailor their strategies accordingly in order to better meet consumer needs and expectations. It's also important to consider how one channel's performance can significantly impact another's, i.e. a social media campaign driving traffic to a website, boosting sales. Multi-channel analysis helps in understanding these synergistic relationships, revealing how different channels collectively contribute to the overall success of a campaign.

As always, a customer-centric approach is key in delivering the best experiences. Brands must focus on providing a seamless and satisfying experience to the customer at every stage of their interaction with them and this principle informs both technological strategy (such as interoperability requirements) and content strategy. I'll be addressing both concepts later in the chapter.

Businesses may need to adapt their models in response to changing technologies, market conditions or consumer needs. Being flexible and adaptable in strategy execution is thus vital, allowing for adjustments based on market feedback. With these principles in mind, we'll look at how they relate to Web 3.0.

The transition between social media and metaverses

The point where social media platforms and virtual worlds intersect is a key consideration when creating a smooth marketing journey. Users should have a seamless, intuitive transition between the two – for example, while watching a product demonstration video on a brand's social media page, the user could click a link to enter a virtual store within the metaverse where they can interact with the product in a lifelike environment. This way, they directly transition from one medium to another, undisrupted. Other techniques for creating seamless entry points into immersive experiences include QR codes and interactive teasers within videos. In fact, videos on social media can serve as trailers or previews for metaverse events or experiences, generating excitement and curiosity and encouraging users to explore the metaverse for the full experience. You can also use appropriate rewards to incentivize users to visit different metaverses.

To bridge the gap effectively, marketers need to ensure that the user interface and experience are consistent across platforms; this includes similar aesthetics, ease of navigation and, of course, consistent branding. The content assets on different platforms should complement each other as well. This synchronization helps with storytelling, keeping the audience engaged in a consistent narrative across platforms.

Cross-platform accessibility is crucial. Users might access social media on their smartphones but enter the metaverse via VR headsets or PCs, so ensuring compatibility and ease of access is key. You may also want to create engaging educational content to introduce your audience to the concept of metaverses, which will help less informed users to step into these new worlds. Focus on educating them about the benefits and experiences awaiting them in the virtual world, along with any practicalities they need to be aware of.

As social media and metaverses thrive on community engagement, marketers should focus on building and nurturing communities that can move fluidly between these spaces, encouraging user-generated content and peer-to-peer interactions that span across them. They should also focus on nurturing cross-metaverse communities and creating shared experiences that encourage users to transition between virtual worlds. The experience of moving between worlds can be gamified, where users can win rewards or virtual collectibles in exchange for their engagement with multiple platforms. Developing unified user profiles or avatars that users can carry across various metaverse platforms is essential for making this possible, helping users maintain a consistent virtual identity.

Speaking of cross-platform use, consider the interoperability requirements that ensure continuity of experience into the future. This involves formulating a future-proof tech stack and strategy. The goal is to create a technological framework and a corresponding strategic plan that can easily adapt to different technologies, platforms or market trends in the future. By doing so, you minimize potential disruptions caused by technological advancements or shifts in user preferences. Also consider accessibility challenges – any marketing strategy should accommodate users with varying levels of technological capabilities to ensure inclusivity and maximum reach. In this context, forming partnerships with tech companies can be a strategic move.

Always consider how data security and privacy will be affected as users move between platforms. While interoperability comes with many benefits, managing and securing data across an interoperable network is inherently more complex than within a single platform. This complexity can lead to oversights and gaps in security protocols, making systems vulnerable to attacks. Interoperability often involves reliance on third-party services and APIs and if these external services are compromised, it can have a cascading effect on the security and functionality of interconnected platforms. The attack surface is also larger in this context; if one platform or application is compromised, it could potentially expose vulnerabilities in interconnected systems, leading to widespread security breaches. As I've said before, a decentralized internet poses unique risks as different platforms may have different standards and no central authority to manage security. So, every organization must do its due diligence and ensure it's doing everything required to mitigate the risks.

Integrating virtual currencies across metaverses and social platforms is another area in which consistency is key. Enabling cross-platform transactions also opens up new opportunities for digital interactions – for example, a user could earn virtual currency on a social media platform through certain activities or promotions and spend it within the metaverse for various services or digital goods, and vice versa. Therefore, businesses need to develop systems where these currencies can be seamlessly transferred and used in different platforms without losing their value or facing compatibility issues. Considering how virtual currencies interact with real-world financial systems is also important, as well as the regulatory requirements involved.

Communications as gateways

Email, messaging apps and other communication channels serve as gateways, guiding users in, out and between digital environments. In terms of onboarding, companies can use these channels to invite users to enter a Web 3.0 experience – for example, a user may receive an email with a so-called deep link that directly transports them to a specific location or event within the metaverse.

Deep links are a type of hyperlink that instead of directing a user to the homepage of a website or the landing page of an app, takes them to a specific, often contextual, location within it. They're commonly used to make the user experience more efficient and personalized and to increase conversions. An example of a deep link we're all familiar with is when a link in an email takes us directly to a specific product page within an e-commerce app rather than just opening the app's homepage. In this context, reducing the number of steps needed to reach a specific destination increases the chances of users taking the action required at that destination.

Deep links are essential for integrating experiences across different platforms. If you want to encourage your customers to visit a specific scene within a VR experience, send them there using a deep link; don't expect them to navigate to it from a different part of the experience.

Leveraging data from user interactions within the metaverse allows companies to send out personalized messages, suggesting content, events or activities within the metaverse that align with their interests and previous activities. It also assists with the cross-promotion of different virtual experiences – for example, a user engaged in one virtual world might receive communications about another related or complementary experience, encouraging exploration and engagement across multiple platforms.

Messaging apps can provide real-time customer support within metaverse environments, enhancing user experiences. They allow for real-time, personalized communication, enabling users to receive immediate assistance. This is particularly beneficial in complex environments where users might require quick help to navigate or understand certain features. It also means that users don't have to leave the platform to seek help, letting them stay engaged in the environment without interruption. Of course, chatbots can be integrated for automating preliminary support.

Through messaging apps, users can receive continuous support post-experience. If this is orchestrated in a way so that they can access support without re-entering the experience, they'll appreciate the convenience. Finally, communications allow brands to follow up with their audience after their participation in virtual experiences, prompting further action.

Content strategies in the metaverse

Content is still king in the metaverse. So, what do marketers need to consider when building a content strategy for this environment? A fundamental point to keep in mind is that if your audience wanted static content, they wouldn't engage with the metaverse, so keep the concept of interactivity at the forefront of your mind and come up with as many creative ways as you can for how your audience can experience it. Remember, even ads can be interactive today and businesses will need to innovate, finding new ways for consumers to engage with the metaverse counterparts of their standard ads.

In earlier chapters I spoke about the different types of metaverse content that businesses are developing. To recap, they include games and open-ended experiences in virtual worlds; virtual events, stores and exhibitions; branded NFTs and other digital assets; virtual product placements; and graphical assets. In the future, VR technology will advance to make content more realistic through tactile sensation and AI may even advance to the point where it can create AR and VR experiences. For now, creating immersive content requires specialist expertise, but brands including Adobe are developing tools that allow people with no technical background to create interactive content.

Creating high-quality, innovative metaverse content will allow businesses to position themselves as forward-thinking and technologically advanced and this is going to be essential amid the vast competition. Not only will businesses be competing against each other, they'll also be competing against user-generated content, which makes up the majority of metaverse content. That's another reason it's vital to leverage users' enthusiasm for generating content and seek out potential collaborative partnerships.

For businesses that are yet to establish a strong presence in the metaverse, the use of sponsored and branded content can play a pivotal role in gaining visibility. Currently, the metaverse attracts specific segments, particularly those interested in technology, gaming and digital innovation. Businesses can use sponsored and branded content to target these niche groups effectively, tailoring their messaging and experiences to the interests and behaviours of these users. We'll look at an example of this in Chapter 18. Creating content that resonates with these audiences in particular is going to be important in the early days; if or when the metaverse starts to attract a wider audience, this will need revisiting.

Partnerships with influencers are going to be just as important in Web 3.0 as now. The concept goes hand in hand with the decentralized nature of Web 3.0, where trust is a paramount concern for users. Influencers, having built communities based on trust and authenticity, can play a vital role in bridging the gap between brands and consumers, their endorsements lending credibility to products and services within these new digital spaces.

Another vital principle is that marketers will need to make content social. Some consider the metaverse an extension of social media as we know it today, which means it will be crucial to create content that provides social interaction. This is facilitated through multiplayer games and other collaborative projects and challenges that require users to work together, fostering a sense of community and teamwork. Integrating metaverse experiences with social media platforms also helps in this regard, encouraging users to invite their connections to join them in the virtual world. Marketers can involve the community in decision-making processes related to the virtual space through feedback, polls or community meetings. This helps users feel invested in the environment and business, fostering a stronger sense of community and loyalty.

What about written content? Will it still be relevant? Its prominence will reduce but there will still be use cases in which marketers need it. Blogs will still exist, at least in the beginning, but they will need to contain interactive elements or come to life through VR. We will also likely see regular content, such as long-form written content and static images, being used as part of new experiences. For example, users may read blogs from within a VR experience, or virtual libraries may be created where users can read virtual copies of e-books or guides with their virtual hands, feeling the pages between their virtual fingers. (This is just an example and would not necessarily catch on; the physical world is here for those that want to read books, after all.) In addition, copywriting will still be necessary in order to engage users in the first place and to guide communications via email and other media. The need for scriptwriting will grow as brands will focus on storytelling more than ever before, so writers won't become obsolete.

Coming back to the point about interactivity, content should be personalized and users should be able to customize it where applicable. In concrete terms, this will include simple things like avatar customization through to the modification of virtual spaces, such as rooms, property or entire landscapes, as well as the narratives that accompany these experiences. In addition, brands can dynamically generate content that responds to user interactions, creating immersive narratives that evolve in real-time.

There will also be AI-driven customization which can include recommending activities, auto-adjusting environments based on user behaviour, or providing personalized NPC interactions. AI enables NPCs to make complex decisions based on various data points, including previous user behaviour and existing rules. As a result, they can actually assess situations and respond accordingly instead of sticking to a script, and the more advanced models can detect emotions based on facial expressions and tone of voice. This ensures a unique experience for every user – and one that feels more genuine, where NPCs show empathy or join users in celebrating their wins. Similarly, brands can use AI-driven 'staff' that serve as virtual guides, offering assistance and information to users navigating virtual spaces.

Finally, as I've mentioned, storytelling can take on new dimensions in the metaverse. Content strategies should leverage the unique capabilities of the platforms to tell stories in innovative, immersive ways, perhaps utilizing non-linear narratives, interactive plot elements and user-driven story development.

Conclusion

To summarize, the metaverse represents a new paradigm for integrated marketing, allowing brands to blur the lines between social media, communications and content strategies. The future of marketing in Web 3.0 lies in the seamless integration of these elements, ensuring that all parts of the marketing mix are joined together to create a holistic and engaging brand experience. The metaverse is an evolving space and strategies should be designed with scalability and adaptability in mind; this means being open to evolving trends in technology, user preferences and the metaverse ecosystem itself.

A content strategy for the metaverse requires a blend of creativity, technical understanding and user experience design. Content should have a strong social focus and be as interactive as possible; even if you aren't already implementing the more advanced technologies characteristic of Web 3.0, start thinking ahead and planning how you can make your existing content formats more interactive.

Overall, the opportunities are endless, but it's crucial to make sure that every aspect of your strategy is interconnected.

14

The changing face of search

AI, NLP, IoT and speech-recognition technologies are transforming the way people search for information – and the way search engines provide it. Search algorithms are becoming more advanced, with better contextual understanding, people are using conversational AI tools such as ChatGPT and Google Bard to find information, and voice search is still on the rise. The combination of these factors is highly disruptive, changing marketers' approaches to creating content that ranks well. In this chapter I'll go through some recent developments, how businesses need to adapt and some trends that might be on the horizon.

How query matching is changing

In 2021, Google launched an update to its algorithm called the Multitask Unified Model (MUM), which equips the search engine to handle more complex queries and serve up more relevant results than ever. It's 1,000 times more powerful than its predecessor, BERT, and the plan is for it to handle indexing, ranking and retrieval (in the past, these functions were carried out by different models) (Marius, 2022). What's more, it's trained in 75 languages and can translate between them. Suppose a user was looking for information that wasn't widely available in their native language. They can now search in their native language while the model retrieves information from sources in other languages and translates it for them, giving users access to information they may not have found before.

The model is multimodal, able to understand the context of one form of media in relation to another, such as why an image was chosen to accompany a piece of text. This makes it possible for Google to understand context in a more advanced way than ever before. Combining MUM with the visual search tool, Google Lens, takes things further. Google Lens has been around for a while, but it's now integrated into the Google app and Chrome browser. If you haven't used it before, I'll explain how it works.

The search process begins when a user points their phone's camera at an object, text or scene and Google Lens captures the image (it can also work with previously captured images from the phone's gallery). Using image recognition, the image is analysed and information about it returned. The user can then ask further questions to find exactly what they're looking for. Let's consider an example Google used in the beginning to demonstrate this feature. Suppose a user wanted to repair a broken part on their bike. With Google Lens, they can take a photo of the part and add text such as 'how to fix'. The search results will then return a video tutorial from YouTube, for example, which explains the steps to repair the part (handy if you don't know what the part is called) (Schreiner, 2021).

The tool integrates with other Google services such as Maps, providing even more useful information. For example, if you point your camera at a restaurant, it can show reviews, opening hours and other relevant details. Likewise, if it recognizes a product within an image, it can show where it's available for purchase online.

Google Lens can also recognize text in images through optical character recognition (OCR) technology, which converts text in images into machine-readable text. This lets users take a photo of a piece of text in another language and instantly get a translation.

Such examples demonstrate how convenient these alternative methods of searching can be compared with the traditional keyword search. However, these advancements bring challenges for marketers. Zero-click searches have been increasing due to the likes of featured snippets, which help users find what they need directly in the search results. An analysis of 5.1 trillion Google searches from 2020 revealed that only 33.59 per cent of searches led to clicks on organic search results; 64.82 per cent had no follow-up click to another web property. Also note that the rate of zero-click searches is higher on mobile devices (77.22 per cent) (Fishkin, 2021).

This is something marketers have had to consider for a while but with MUM, the accuracy, relevance and completeness of featured snippets and other answer formats is greater and will only improve. The model's ability to understand and interpret complex, conversational queries lets it provide specific answers that closely match the user's intent, and unlike its predecessors, it can integrate information from a variety of sources and formats to provide a more comprehensive answer, mimicking the experience of visiting a webpage. It can also anticipate what information a user might look for next based on their initial query.

All the above factors not only improve the quality of answers, they also make them more likely to be complete and final on the search results page itself. As such, businesses need to change their approach to content creation and SEO to increase their chances of appearing in search engine results pages (SERPs). It's important to be proactive in identifying opportunities to show up in featured snippets and optimize accordingly. Also keep a close eye on the clicks-per-search (CPS) metric – if your content is ranking well but the CPS is low, it's a sign the content needs better optimization (you may also want to optimize for related keywords that have a higher CPS value). In featured snippets, the image displayed isn't always from the same website as the content, so if you optimize your images, that's another way for people to find your website. Schema markup also becomes even more important in light of clickless searches, providing explicit clues to Google about the meaning of the page content.

Focusing on search intent is vital due to the model's ability to understand context. As such, marketers need to delve deeper into why someone is searching for a particular topic and tailor content accordingly. MUM's ability to understand nuanced, complex queries also means that content should address more sophisticated and detailed topics, so marketers should develop content that comprehensively covers a subject, exploring it from various angles and covering a wide range of topics related to the target keyword. Long-tail keywords also become more critical with this advancement.

Using a variety of content formats will be a must and that's not just because of the multimodal nature of MUM; as you know, text-based content will be less dominant as Web 3.0 progresses, so incorporating other formats (especially video) becomes crucial. Video SEO should therefore be a focus, which involves optimizing titles, descriptions, tags and file names and ensuring that videos are accessible and provide value. Video scripts should be optimized because search engines crawl transcripts and closed captions.

In summary, adapting to the MUM update (and its future releases) involves creating richer, more nuanced content that addresses long, complex queries. Marketers should focus more on search intent and diversifying content types (especially towards video). This approach not only aligns with the capabilities of MUM, it also caters to evolving user behaviours.

The impact of generative AI

Despite these search engine advancements, language models including GPT and Bard may disrupt everything. When ChatGPT was released, people were using it to seek information instead of searching on Google. At the time, there was a lot of hype about how search engines may be under threat in future; after all, why wouldn't users opt for the quickest, most efficient way to find information? Instead of browsing the search results hoping to find something relevant, they're served up with a detailed answer immediately. For the time being, ChatGPT isn't always accurate and can't be trusted without fact checking, but it's quite possible that in future, these language models will change the way users search forever. If these tools became the go-to means of finding information, search engines would be compromised since they rely on advertising. However, recent data shows that ChatGPT has only 2 per cent of the traffic Google receives (Goodwin, 2023).

Regardless, user behaviour is set to change as search engines integrate conversational AI (another reason it's going to be so important for content to be optimized for conversational search terms). Until recently, Google Bard wasn't integrated into the search function and was accessed separately, but that's all set to change. Bard is powered by Google's Gemini model and a recent update has made it more powerful than ever. Google Bard had to move fast to compete with the pace of ChatGPT. The search giant even brought Google co-founder Sergey Brin out of retirement to help maximise the AI engine's capability. In the process of rapidly building out a multimodal platform they renamed the product to Gemini (the engine that sits behind it) and have focussed on heavily on a rapid improvement. It's vital for all marketers to stay on top of these changes as they are moving fast and Google is never a business to take you eye off.

It's impossible to say for sure what's coming next, but conversational AI tools are also likely to increase the number of clickless searches. Not only will marketers need to change their approach to content, as mentioned earlier, they'll also need to change their PPC strategy. This can include creating conversational, personalized ads to improve engagement and of course optimizing for voice queries. Ads may also integrate chatbot functionality to encourage users to enter into conversation; from there, they can provide immediate assistance or answers to prospects, potentially leading to higher conversion rates. Moreover, it's important to enhance website UX to ensure that when users do click through, they find what they're looking for easily.

With the rise of clickless searches, having a strong brand presence can ensure that users seek out your business directly. This highlights the importance of brand marketing, developing immersive experiences and diversifying the channels you use, made possible by the variety that comes with Web 3.0.

Aside from these adaptations, marketers should familiarize themselves with the other impacts AI is having on paid search and how to make the most of it. For example, automated bidding strategies analyse large sets of data to determine the most effective bid for each ad based on factors like time of day, user demographics and past behaviour. This leads to more efficient use of advertising budgets, as bids are optimized for the highest possible ROAS. Dynamic ad creation and optimization is another vital tool. To recap, AI can automatically create and test different variations of ads to determine which ones perform the best. This includes optimizing ad copy, images and calls-to-action based on real-time feedback.

The rise of voice search

Combined with IoT technology, voice search is bringing about significant changes in the process of search ranking. First of all, voice searches tend to be more conversational and longer than text-based searches, shifting the focus from traditional keyword-based SEO to natural language- and question-based content. After all, search algorithms are increasingly focusing on user experience, which includes the relevance of answers, the speed of delivering them and the ease of interaction (especially important in voice search). So, with voice search, there's a shift from keyword density to the quality of content.

Since voice searches often seek direct answers, algorithms prioritize content that provides clear, concise and accurate information. In the past, businesses could rely on their FAQ sections to improve their rankings, but this is no longer the case. In 2023, Google announced that FAQ results (from FAQPage structured data markup) will show in search results only if they are from well-known, authoritative government and health websites. It also made changes to the way HowTo structured data is used. This markup is used for content that explains how to do something, walking visitors through the necessary steps (not just in text form, it's also used for video, images, etc.). From now on, HowTo structured data will be shown for desktop users only. As such, you need to take other steps to account for mobile devices, especially since the majority of voice searches are done using mobile devices. (You should still include HowTo structured data on the relevant sections of your mobile site as Google uses the mobile version as the basis for indexing (Mueller, 2023).)

Since FAQs and how-to content won't do the trick anymore, what can marketers do to provide the concise, direct answers that help in ranking for voice search? First, they should develop question-based content that the audience is looking for and provide concise answers. Headings should be in question form and contain relevant long-tail keywords – for example, 'When is the best time to book cheap flights to Berlin?'

As most voice and local searches are done on mobile devices, websites must be mobile-friendly, with responsive design and easily navigable interfaces. Page-loading speed is a critical factor for SEO, especially for mobile and voice search, so this must be optimized; tools like Google PageSpeed Insights can analyse and improve loading time.

As I've said before, voice searches are frequently used for local queries. As such, businesses that need to promote products or services in specific locations must ensure their listings are up to date and accurate on platforms like Google Business Profile, and actively manage local customer reviews. They should also integrate location-specific keywords into their website content, as well as create content related to local events and other local topics, increasing their local relevance.

A study by Semrush gives us more insights about how to rank well. First, 70 per cent of answers returned from voice searches occupied a SERP feature, 60 per cent of which returned a featured snippet result, so keep in mind the tips I mentioned earlier on this topic. Answers were also readable and understandable by the average 15-year-old. (Readability has always been vital and this study proves its importance for voice search as well.) For Google Home and Home Mini searches, backlink anchors and keywords were included in a title matching the query in more than 50 per cent of cases. Also note that the average answer length was 41 words. As such, it's common to give web pages a headline phrased as a common question, then give a short answer in around 40 words straight after, followed by detailed information on the subject (Andrienko, 2019).

The future of voice search

We know what we need to do to rank for voice search at the moment, but where are things heading? A few trends are likely to develop in the near future, the most obvious being that speech recognition and NLP will improve, increasing accuracy and contextual understanding. Search engines will then provide more relevant results than ever.

As voice search and voice assistants grow in popularity, consumers will want voice to be the means of controlling other tasks, so voice-enabled chatbots may become the norm and we may see them integrated into ads more often, as mentioned. We'll also see them being integrated with apps more often.

Hyperlocal searches are also increasing. These queries are extremely specific to a small, local area, often conducted by people looking for businesses, services or events within their immediate vicinity. This goes beyond just city- or town-level searches to target specific neighbourhoods, streets or even parts of a street. For example, a search for 'coffee shops near King's Cross station' is hyperlocal, targeting a very specific area (that's why hyperlocal searches are closely integrated with geo-targeting and beacon technology). Optimizing for hyperlocal search involves including specific neighbourhood names, landmarks and local details in website content, local listings and metadata. Providing such specific solutions can increase conversation rates as they provide precisely what a consumer needs, exactly when they need it and, in time, this builds loyalty.

Voice assistants can already recognize individual voices and adapt to user preferences and this will only become more precise over time. Advancements will likely involve a more nuanced understanding of individual speech patterns, accents and even the emotional tone behind spoken commands. As a result, voice assistants will evolve from being simple command-based tools to more intuitive, interactive personal aids.

What is a search engine?

One final point to keep in mind here is that while this chapter has been focused on the future of search engines, not all users are starting their searches here. In fact, a high percentage today conduct their searches from TikTok, YouTube and other search and content engines. This is likely to continue as the enrichment of the internet continues and so should be a key piece of thinking in your Web3 search strategy.

Senior Vice President Prabhakar Raghavan, who runs Google's Knowledge & Information organization, stated, 'In our studies, something like almost 40 per cent of young people, when they're looking for a place for lunch, they don't go to Google Maps or Search, they go to TikTok or Instagram' (Perez, 2022).

Conclusion

Keeping up with changes to search algorithms is essential as user behaviours continue to evolve. Marketers should already be optimizing content for voice search and the latest updates to MUM, while keeping a lookout for the ongoing impacts that conversational AI will have. A key change that is going to be important no matter what happens with the likes of Bard is to diversify content formats because, as I said in the last chapter, the growth of the metaverse could vastly reduce the importance of long-form written content. So, diversifying not only makes content preferable by the current algorithms, it future - proofs your efforts in the long run.

Notes

Andrienko, O (2019) Voice search study: Factors influencing search engine rankings in 2019. Semrush. 5 June, www.semrush.com/blog/voice-search-study/ (archived at https://perma.cc/S5RE-5U5P)

Fishkin, R (2021) In 2020, two thirds of Google searches ended without a click. SparkToro. 22 March, https://sparktoro.com/blog/in-2020-two-thirds-of-google-searches-ended-without-a-click/ (archived at https://perma.cc/BLG5-MJQK)

Goodwin, D (2023) No, ChatGPT isn't stealing Google's search market share. Search Engine Land. 9 November https://searchengineland.com/no-chatgpt-isnt-stealing-googles-search-market-share-434465 (archived at https://perma.cc/Z3P4-8WZQ)

Marius, H (2022) RIP BERT: Google's MUM is coming. Medium. 10 January, https://towardsdatascience.com/rip-bert-googles-mum-is-coming-cb3becd9670f (archived at https://perma.cc/A8YC-GXDL)

Mueller, J (2023) Changes to HowTo and FAQ rich results. Google. 8 August, https://developers.google.com/search/blog/2023/08/howto-faq-changes (archived at https://perma.cc/4HL3-M5MX)

Perez, S (2022) Google exec suggests Instagram and TikTok are eating into Google's core products, Search and Maps. Techcrunch. 12 July, https://techcrunch.com/2022/07/12/google-exec-suggests-instagram-and-tiktok-are-eating-into-googles-core-products-search-and-maps/?guccounter=2 (archived at https://perma.cc/RT8W-EANV)

Schreiner, M (2021) Multimodal AI: MUM is the future of Google search. The Decoder. 30 September, https://the-decoder.com/multimodal-ai-mum-is-the-future-of-google-search/ (archived at https://perma.cc/T9D4-5ZDH)

15

Building meaningful content strategies in Web 3.0

It's no longer enough to view content as a one-way street where information is simply disseminated to a passive audience. Web 3.0 demands a redefinition of content itself – it's now about creating an ecosystem where users are not just consumers but active participants. This shift requires brands to think creatively about embedding their presence into various content forms. Like I've said before, examples include integrating a brand into a VR game in a way that adds value to the user experience or using AR to bring a product to life in the consumer's living room. The keyword here is value – that's the purpose of all content.

Given the omnipresent nature of content these days, there are endless opportunities to infuse brand messaging into it. However, it's important to make sure this integration is seamless, enhancing rather than interrupting the user experience. In other words, branding should feel like a natural part of the experience, not an add-on. This requires a deep understanding of the platform and its users, as well as creative ways to weave brand elements into the content.

In this chapter we delve into the heart of creating meaningful content strategies in the Web 3.0 era, focusing on how brands can infuse their message into this new, synergistic landscape. We'll look at the keys to making content successful, the ways our interaction with content is changing and how marketers need to adapt.

The pillars of successful content in Web 3.0

In my first book, *Digital Marketing Strategy*, I shared the models I have built throughout my career to ensure you can deliver high-impact content. In my second book, *The Digital Marketing Handbook*, I shared smart campaign tips and tricks for ensuring your content resonates and delivers against your goals. Those models and examples are still relevant as we move into Web3, but we need to consider some new angles to ensure we meet consumer needs and changing technological foundations.

Perhaps the most essential principle is relevance. At the heart of the matter is understanding your audience and what they want and need and displaying it in the right place at the right time. Looking back at the case studies we've discussed, we can see how companies bridge the gap between seemingly unrelated concepts in order to broaden their reach. Consider Wendy's meat freezer smashing concept in collaboration with *Fortnite*; they simply found a relevant item/concept within the existig platform (the in-game restaurants and their freezers) and tied that to their offering and messaging – burgers made from meat that's fresh and not frozen. Their messaging was part of the entertainment and not an add-on. The user experience – of gaming – was not disrupted. The campaign was contextually relevant and seamlessly positioned for users to engage with it.

As I've said, content should be fun, educational or both. Many types of Web 3.0 content lay the foundation for entertainment by default, such as games and gamified storytelling – and incorporating game mechanics into storytelling, where users can earn rewards, achieve goals and progress through narrative layers in a gamified manner.

Another key principle of successful content is that it's shareable and, as always, this is determined by the value it provides as well as the practical sharing methods available. In Web 2.0, sharing was all about posting on social media and having social links available for the major social platforms. This was the next step on from having to email someone directly with a link to the URL, as it was in the old days. Likewise, Web 3.0 will come with its own native options, such as sending deep links to metaverse locations. Marketers will need to consider how the user interfaces of each platform will enable sharing and design experiences accordingly.

The role of community in Web 3.0 will be advantageous in terms of sharing, which I'll elaborate on shortly. In addition, multiplayer games are shareable by nature, so consider what experiences you can create that encourage the participation of multiple users. You can also gamify and incentivize the act of sharing content, and there are many new ways to do that thanks to Web 3.0 technology, such as token-based incentive programmes where users gain rewards for engagement and participation.

As I touched on before, it's important to make content shareable across platforms and between metaverse worlds and social media channels. (Campaigns that encourage users to post content from the metaverse on their social accounts also make use of the principle of exclusivity, if they're the first within their community to engage with something new.)

Next, your content should be different. It should stand out as unique. Marketing within these new contexts is still a novelty, but as more businesses start using the new channels, it's going to be more important to think outside the box. This doesn't mean reinventing the wheel with each campaign, but content should draw people's attention and inspire curiosity – and something that's been done time and time again won't have such an effect.

AI and generative content

We discussed AI in more detail in Chapter 9, but we can't discuss content for Web3 without touching on AI here. The reason I wanted to interrupt my flow here to make the point is specifically because we are talking about uniqueness. AI for generating content at this stage (early 2024 as I write this) has come a long way in a relatively short time since really hitting the mainstream in late 2022. However, there is still a way to go before we can fully rely on it to create correct, interesting and meaningful pieces that are well written and fit our brand. This isn't to say that it can't be done but that it is not yet a well-established process for most businesses. This is both the technology and the user's understanding of how to optimize the process for the best results. This means that using the same platforms (e.g. ChatGPT) with the same basic prompts has a high risk of delivering generic answers that, if used as brand content or the basis of a content strategy, will result in a significant volume of similar content, eroding brand value and consumer trust. Marketers must be wary of this and ensure they do not fall into this trap. Anyway, back to the chapter...

So, what can you offer that's unique, within your brand's metaverse world and elsewhere? Awe-inspiring graphics, unique navigation methods and interactive features, or even the way users engage with content and each other, can make an impact. Collaborate with artists, designers, influencers or other brands to bring in fresh perspectives and unique content (while broadening your reach). You can also host exclusive virtual events, offer unique digital products or specialized interactive experiences that are deeply immersive. Keep your brand's metaverse world dynamic and evolving, with regular updates, new features and seasonal changes. Users may have endless immersive experiences to choose from in future, so brands need to keep them coming back for more.

Non-fungible tokens

NFTs are another option for creating something unique. Creating a story or emotional connection around the NFT can increase its appeal; this could involve the history behind it, its creation process, or its significance in the broader context of the brand's journey. Storytelling in general is a key to offering something distinct and it can inject life into any context. For example, global water management and processing company Nalco Water worked with creative agency Sector 5 Digital to develop content about its services. It wanted to make an impression on clients visiting its facilities that would include 'jaw-dropping moments' while addressing their business requirements. The companies worked together to create compelling narratives about how Nalco Water helped clients overcome challenges and this was presented using 360 and 3D projection. This shows how experiential content is expanding beyond the obvious scenarios we might expect (The Glimpse Group, n.d.).

User-generated content and community are fundamental, interrelated pillars of Web 3.0. Within the metaverse and Web 3.0 overall are many niche subcultures and brands will need to identify which ones they need to reach and target them appropriately, using content that resonates with them. Creators are often individuals who are highly engaged in these digital communities; they could be artists, writers, bloggers, vloggers or any content creators who are active in online spaces, especially those interested in blockchain technologies, cryptocurrencies and NFTs.

Brands should research and identify communities and platforms where their target audience is active. Before launching a UGC campaign, it's crucial to establish a presence and engage authentically within these communities. This could involve participating in discussions, providing insights and discovering community norms and interests. Again, this helps brands to get the message across in a way that's natural for the context.

Brands should use their existing channels to amplify selected UGC, giving credit to the creators. This not only showcases the content but also strengthens the community by highlighting member contributions. The goal is to maintain an active and vibrant community where UGC continues to flourish, so keep members engaged through regular interactions, updates and new incentives. Also encourage co-creation and collaboration; this could be through contests or projects where community members can build upon each other's work.

A key question to keep in mind to gauge whether your content is unique is this: 'Is this content differentiated enough to cut through the noise and get my audience's attention?' Keep revisiting this question as markets, platforms and technologies evolve.

Finally, make sure content is on brand and authentic. It can be easy to get carried away (especially when storytelling is involved), but if the content ideas are irrelevant to, or incompatible with, the brand, they serve no purpose. Regarding authenticity, this is funda-mental for Gen Z and to a world that values decentralization. Again, this highlights the importance of content being in the right place – in front of the right audience. If it appears in a community or environment where it shouldn't be, consumers will take note; they'll put their guard up, potentially trust the brand less and ulti-mately the brand's reputation may be damaged. This ties in with a point I made before about using emerging technologies judiciously: don't use them haphazardly, just for the sake of it – use them in a way that aligns with your business model and provides strategic advantage.

New ways of interacting with content

The ways in which people interact with content will change dramati-cally. In future, content will no longer be static. Through the likes of interactive storytelling (also known as storyliving) and personaliza-tion, it will almost take on a life of its own. It's becoming more common for brands to let users influence the narrative of storified experiences and choose their own adventures. This is common with open metaverse worlds, VR, AR and interactive video formats, but it's not restricted to these immersive content types. For example, the process of gathering customer feedback could even be interactive and feature storytelling elements, boosting engagement so that businesses can collect comprehensive data more easily.

The level of interaction afforded by interactive storytelling creates a deeply personal connection between the user and the content. The content may also be different each time they interact with it based on their choices, allowing them to re-experience it and engage further. Leveraging data and AI, Web 3.0 storytelling can offer personalized experiences to different users, adapting to their preferences, past interactions and choices within the narrative. What's more, interac-tive elements provide a whole new set of data points that can help marketers gain deep insights into consumer behaviour.

This new way of relating to customers can seem less pushy compared with more traditional marketing tactics. These days, it's important to reach customers in a way that gets past their defences – defences that are up due to the endless information and marketing material that they're bombarded with every day. Whatever the content format, it provides an opportunity for brands to have a dialogue with their audience, enabling meaningful relationships based on trust.

Blockchain technology supports interactive storytelling. For example, smart contracts can automate certain story elements based on audience interactions or other triggers, leading to dynamic storylines that evolve based on predetermined rules or audience engagement. There are many formulae used to break down narrative structure into components and researchers have been experimenting with blockchain to mechanize the process (Maxwell et al., 2017). As such, aspects of a story, such as characters, plot elements and settings, can be tokenized, allowing users to own, trade or invest in specific parts of a story.

Content is at the heart of Web 3.0 communities, making it a vital medium for distribution. The decentralized platforms supporting some communities use blockchain to enable collaborative storytelling, where multiple users guide the narrative together. Through tokenized voting systems, audience members can influence story outcomes, character fates or narrative arcs. This can lead to richer and more diverse content, as it's being created and shared by a wide and varied community rather than being dictated by a few dominant participants.

There are also dedicated, decentralized platforms for collaborative storytelling, such as StoryCo. These platforms are designed to decentralize filmmaking and intellectual property and involve fans in the creative process to improve the project's success. Previously called StoryDAO, the company received $6 million in seed capital from a range of crypto investment firms and in 2023 released its first collaborative, interactive story experience, known as *The Disco Ball*. The experience was produced by Kyle Killen, writer of the *Halo* TV series. The community collaborates to develop the main character's journey and contributors earn a stake in the project's success (Thompson, 2023).

The technological foundations are there, so it will be interesting to see how brands start decentralizing the narratives built for experiential content, whether that's for a gamified VR experience or collaborating on brand narratives. Thanks to the interoperability of Web 3.0, stories may also span various platforms and formats, offering a more expansive narrative experience. For instance, a story might begin on a social platform, extend into an interactive game and conclude in a VR environment.

Consumer behaviour and trends

As indicated above, consumer behaviours are changing considerably. Marketers need to understand these shifts deeply and keep tabs on evolving trends in order to reach consumers in the optimal way. In this section I'll discuss some data relating to the concepts in the previous section, among others.

We know that emerging technologies like VR are significantly impacting consumer behaviour, particularly among Gen Z and Gen Alpha. For these digital natives, immersiveness is not just a nice-to-have, it's expected. Research by Deloitte supports this trend and also shows that there's significant interest in VR among Millennials. 29 per cent of Gen Z and Millennials combined are using VR to visit different locations, such as foreign cities and historical sites, 26 per cent are using it to meet friends and family, 24 per cent are using it to attend live events and for learning purposes, and 23 per cent are using it to shop for clothes and household items (Auxler and Arbanas, 2023). Businesses whose audiences consist of these consumers must align with this shift.

It is important to be aware that consumers are still sceptical about projects involving cryptocurrency due to its volatility. In addition, we're quite a way off from the days when using crypto for purchases will be the norm. Users need to understand wallets, private keys and so on, and this may be second nature to many members of Gen Z, but it's still a barrier to widespread adoption. That's why it's so important to be judicious about which Web 3.0 technologies are suitable for your brand specifically.

Even if cryptocurrency doesn't appeal to your audience, other forms of virtual currency are growing in popularity. In research by Hubspot, 27 per cent of consumers said they would be more likely to use a platform if they received virtual currency for doing so. In addition, more than 50 per cent of consumers that had ever bought virtual currency or items had done so within the three months leading up to the study (2022). The study also indicated that only 34 per cent of cryptocurrency owners have made a purchase using crypto. So, even if your audience isn't ready to go all in, the option to earn crypto in exchange for sharing content, for example, may still appeal to them. Using virtual currency and items within your content strategy and the experiences you develop is definitely worth considering; there's growing demand for it and it's good for engagement (Forsey, 2022).

As I've said before, consumers will have greater ownership and control over their personal data in Web 3.0 and this shift means they can choose what data they share, with whom and under what circumstances. They'll also be able to revoke access when they want to. As a result, consumers will engage with content that respects their privacy choices, leading to a more trust-based relationship with brands. Marketers will have less access to broad swathes of consumer data and this highlights the need to focus more on creating high-quality content that appeals to the target audience on a deep level rather than relying on extensive data-driven targeting. This goes hand in hand with the changes we're seeing in search engines; developing high-quality content is therefore essential on many fronts.

Engaging consumers through community-driven content and interactions can compensate for the reduced ability to leverage extensive personal data. Marketers will need to focus on long-term objectives and look beyond immediate performance. After all, Rome wasn't built in a day – communities take time to build.

Conclusion

We need to redefine content as a two-way interaction between brands and consumers. When infusing marketing messaging into Web 3.0 platforms and communities, it's important to do so in a way that's natural and non-intrusive; in a way that complements the user experience. It's also essential that content is relevant, shareable, authentic, on-brand and unique (NFTs and UGC are just two approaches that lend themselves well to creating something novel and exclusive).

A successful content strategy hinges on understanding and embracing the decentralized, community-driven nature of this new era. Brands must engage authentically with relevant communities, create appealing incentive structures and facilitate a space where creators feel valued and empowered. Storytelling is another fundamental in creating unique content that aligns with the changes in how people interact with it. Finally, marketers must keep their finger on the pulse of emerging and evolving trends in order to create the most effective content as we move ahead into this new era. VR is already mainstream among Gen Z consumers – who knows how soon we'll be saying the same about crypto and DAOs?

Notes

Auxler, B and Arbanas, J (2023) While we wait for the metaverse to materialize, young people are already there. Deloitte Insights. 27 July, www2.deloitte.com/us/en/insights/industry/technology/gen-z-and-millennials-are-metaverse-early-adopters.html (archived at https://perma.cc/KVN6-LT87)

Forsey, C (2022) How Web3 technology will impact the future of consumer trends [expert insights]. Hubspot. 11 July, https://blog.hubspot.com/marketing/web3-consumer-trends (archived at https://perma.cc/J6PR-BD83)

Maxwell, D, Speed, C and Pschetz, L (2017) Story blocks: Reimagining narrative through the blockchain. University of York. *The International Journal of Research into New Media Technologies*. pp. 79–97. ISSN 1748-7382. https://eprints.whiterose.ac.uk/115257/1/storyblocks_forPURE.pdf (archived at https://perma.cc/9EZN-5439)

The Glimpse Group (n.d.) Engaging stakeholders and clients with experiential storytelling. www.theglimpsegroup.com/case-studies/enganging-stakeholders-and-clients-with-experiential-storytelling (archived at https://perma.cc/WC2Y-2BE5)

Thompson, C (2023) Hollywood in Web3: StoryCo raises $6m to decentralize storytelling. Coindesk. 26 January, www.coindesk.com/web3/2023/01/26/hollywood-in-web3-storyco-raises-6m-to-decentralize-storytelling/ (archived at https://perma.cc/7AX4-RVPC)

PART THREE

Marketing in Web3

16

How consumers will behave in Web3

Gartner delayed its predictions about enterprise use of decentralized applications, with many of its clients prioritizing the use of AI for the next couple of years (Paul, 2024). But even if it takes longer than expected for Web 3.0 technologies to be adopted at scale, consumer attitudes, behaviours and expectations are driving change. In this chapter we'll explore these shifts, among other emerging trends that are setting the stage for Web 3.0.

Trust in brands vs communities

In the Web 2.0 era, trust was predominantly vested in brands and corporations. Users relied on established names like Google, Facebook and Amazon for various online services, trusting them to protect their data, provide reliable services and ensure a safe online environment. This model had its limitations, including privacy concerns and issues related to censorship. With the rise of decentralized technologies, trust is increasingly shifting from centralized entities to communities and protocols. This shift has profound implications for how individuals interact with digital platforms and make decisions about their online engagements. Users are now placing their trust in code instead of centralized authorities. This is in line with the principle of 'code is law', i.e. smart contracts and dApps (executing functions without intermediaries, with users trusting the code and the blockchain's transparency and immutability).

---

dAPPS

A decentralized application (dApp) is a type of distributed, open-source software application that runs on a peer-to-peer (P2P) blockchain network.

The term 'code is law' was initially used in 1999 by American lawyer Lawrence Lessig in his book *Code and Other Laws of Cyberspace*. The book explores issues with this principle and suggests that regulation is still necessary; in fact, the code itself will act as a regulator. He argues that people commonly view regulation in black-and-white terms – it's there or it's not. However, despite minimal government intervention, the interests of programmers will prevail and end up regulating cyberspace. Programmers may not share the same values as the general public, such as privacy, therefore we can't be sure that our collective values will underpin the code that governs the internet. Lessig suggests that code and traditional regulation must work together, with the code itself being regulated. Other issues include the fact that code cannot account for every possible eventuality; as such, a self-executing contract leaves no room for human discretion.

These views were expressed some time ago, but the principle of code as law is still controversial today. With that said, third-party audits of smart contracts are becoming standard practice. They provide users with added confidence in the security, reliability and correctness of the code, ensuring it complies with best practices. It's the responsibility of both developers and users to ensure smart contracts are audited and the process typically involves both manual assessments and automated tools.

As you know, community governance is a central tenet of this new paradigm, with DAOs enabling collective decision-making among token holders. The census of the community then becomes the source of trust. In addition, the interoperability among platforms fosters trust in the sense that users have more flexibility and control over their digital assets and identities as they are not locked into a single platform.

Despite the potential drawbacks of putting our trust in such models, it's clear that internet users are leaning towards them and new regulations will be enforced to strengthen confidence in new platforms and protocols.

The rise of DeSoc and decentralized social networks

'DeSoc' stands for decentralized society. The concept is an overarching term which expands on the principles mentioned above. It involves several key tenets: decentralized governance, decentralized finance, decentralized communication and decentralized production. We've already discussed governance and DeFi is coming up later, so let's examine the others.

Decentralized production enables more transparent, efficient and democratic production processes, driven by communities and peer-to-peer transactions. It enables better social and environmental conditions throughout the supply chain: under a centralized model, businesses can get away with exploiting workers and engaging in unsustainable practices with little accountability, but a decentralized model ensures transparency. As such, it makes 'greenwashing' (the practice of looking like one is being sustainable just to win over consumers, without backing it up with real action) redundant.

Of course, it's not just about the literal production of goods – it applies to services and digital content and we've looked at several examples in prior chapters. Musicians, artists and other creators can distribute their work directly to their audiences without relying on intermediaries; as a result, they benefit from more creative control and fairer compensation. Another intriguing example is the application of decentralization in the energy industry, where users can engage in peer-to-peer energy trading (for example, trading among households that have solar panels). This could potentially encourage more widespread use of renewables.

Now for decentralized communication. In Web 2.0, communication channels were limited and controlled by governments and large corporations. Of course, a key drawback here is the control and manipulation of information, at least when it comes to social media. There's also the fact that users are subject to questionable practices made possible by the algorithms (i.e. being shown content that incites polarization), not to mention the mental health consequences that vulnerable individuals have experienced.

TikTok has been heavily criticized as its algorithm sends users down a rabbit hole, quickly bombarding them with similar yet increasingly extreme content on topics such as self-harm and suicidal ideation (Upper Echelon, 2024). Due to concerns about the effects this has on young people's mental health, several studies have been conducted to examine the potential consequences of engaging with mental health-related content. One study by Amnesty International showed that after engaging with just one piece of content on the topic of mental health, users were rapidly bombarded with increasingly extreme and damaging content that openly promoted self-harm, or worse. 'Rapidly' meant within 20 minutes in some tests; in others, it took only three minutes (Amnesty International, 2023).

The Wall Street Journal also investigated this principle. It found that within minutes, 93 per cent of the content displayed was depressive; the remaining 7 per cent was mostly ads (WSJ, 2021).

The major platforms are designed to be addictive, thus compromising our attention and productivity.

Decentralized social networks overcome such problems. Founded on blockchain technology with no central server, they're designed to be transparent and give users more control over the content they engage with. Platforms such as Mastodon enable users to filter out topics they don't want to engage with while still providing the opportunity to engage with a global audience. As such, Mastodon retains its function as a tool for networking while eliminating various ethical issues. Steemit is another decentralized social media platform, based in the US. As well as providing networking functionality, users can earn the cryptocurrency known as STEEM by publishing content as well as engaging with others' content.

Another key difference with decentralized social media is that users are no longer the product. Currently, they gain free access in exchange for handing over their personal information, which is then used for profit. Again, marketers will need to be more creative in incentivizing users to share their data, as well as leverage the power of community and strong branding. Customers will also have the opportunity to monetize their own data.

Other principles central to DeSoc include using tamper-proof records of user identities. These records are designed to be resistant to manipulation and could help increase the ROI of advertising budgets. Of course, businesses want their ads to be shown to actual humans and not bots, yet inaccurate ad placements happen all the time. Blockchain can help to verify profiles, potentially increasing return on ad spend.

Decentralization also fosters the development of grassroots movements and community-driven initiatives, encouraging consumers to participate in causes they believe in as well as directly support content creators and artists through micropayments and token-based tipping. DeSoc envisions a society where a variety of ideologies can coexist, due to the lack of centralized control.

Open source has been a fundamental driving force shaping the development, ethos and principles of this decentralized and blockchain-powered paradigm. Major blockchain platforms like Ethereum are open source, allowing anyone to view, modify and contribute to their codebases. Multiple contributors worldwide collaborate on code repositories and decisions are made collectively within communities, which mirrors the open-source philosophy of transparent, collaborative, community-driven development. Open-source principles also encourage healthy competition and innovation, driving rapid improvement of the given ecosystem.

Of course, the reality of a decentralized society depends on overcoming various challenges, such as the need or widespread adoption, and the aforementioned issues about regulation. Regardless, DeSoc and decentralized social networks are trends to watch.

The arrival of DeFi

The growing interest in DeFi and cryptocurrencies is a hallmark of consumer behaviour in Web 3.0. More people are exploring alternatives to traditional banking and financial services, opting for decentralized platforms that give users access to financial services like lending, borrowing and trading, all conducted on blockchain networks. One of the primary attractions of DeFi is the potential for higher returns compared with conventional financial systems. Users can earn interest, rewards and governance tokens by participating in various DeFi protocols and dApps. This potential for financial growth has drawn considerable attention from investors and users alike.

There was a slump in 2023, but it appears that DeFi will continue to grow. Total Value Locked (TVL) is a pivotal metric within this space, reflecting the adoption and scale of a project. It calculates the total value of assets locked within smart contracts associated with a particular DeFi platform. In 2023, TVL across the board experienced a notable drop, leading to concerns about the overall health of the ecosystem. This decline was particularly alarming as it signalled a departure from the higher TVL figures seen in the sector before the drop. Several factors contributed to this decline. Regulatory uncertainties cast a shadow over the sector, while various security breaches and hacks eroded trust as users questioned the safety of their assets within smart contracts. In addition, the entire blockchain space experienced a slowdown in 2023, impacting the activities and growth of DeFi projects.

Despite the challenges faced in 2023, DeFi has recovered. Revenue in the DeFi market is forecast to reach $26,170.0 million during 2024 and is expected to show a CAGR of 9.07 per cent between now and 2028. As a result, the projected revenue for 2028 is $37,040.0 million. By 2028, the total number of users is forecast to be 22.09 million. Currently, the US is the largest market (Statista, 2023).

In the previous chapter I mentioned how Gen Z are driving VR adoption; this demographic is also interested in cryptocurrency and DeFi and may influence widespread adoption. This topic was explored in a conversation between Nasdaq and Gracy Chen, managing director of crypto trading platform Bitget. When asked what characteristics of Gen Z may make them more likely to embrace these changes, Chen cites as an important factor the fact that they've been exposed to financial crises. In addition, she points out that their habit of sharing via social media could break down entry barriers and that Gen Z are more likely to support projects that prioritize sustainability and social responsibility (Clarke, 2023).

The tokenization of real-world assets

Another growing trend is the tokenization of real-world assets – the process of representing ownership or rights to physical or tangible assets, such as real estate, art, stocks, commodities or even intellectual property, as digital tokens on a blockchain. For example, a piece of art worth $2 million could be tokenized into 2,000 shares at $1,000 each; this fractional ownership democratizes investment and enhances liquidity. Depending on the asset and its associated smart contract, token holders may receive dividends, rental income or other benefits generated by the asset. Of course, this shift comes with regulatory challenges and requires a robust legal framework to ensure investor protection and compliance with existing financial regulations.

X-to-Earn

X-to-Earn (X2E) apps represent a groundbreaking opportunity to integrate cryptocurrency into users' daily lives, fostering greater engagement with the blockchain ecosystem. As 2024 progresses, it's likely that these earning strategies will proliferate. Among the emerging X-to-Earn strategies gaining significant traction, several stand out as particularly promising. Play-to-Earn, or P2E, turns gaming into profit, enabling users to earn cryptocurrency while enjoying immersive gaming experiences. Gamers can now monetize their skills, assets and in-game achievements, creating a symbiotic relationship between entertainment and financial incentives. Another is

Learn-to-Earn. L2E platforms are revolutionizing education by rewarding users with cryptocurrency for acquiring knowledge and skills. Individuals are then motivated to expand their horizons while reaping the financial benefits.

Move-to-Earn (M2E) leverages the growing emphasis on health and fitness by incentivizing physical activity. Users are encouraged to maintain active lifestyles through wearable devices and apps, earning cryptocurrency as they achieve fitness milestones. This innovative approach promotes well-being and financial gain simultaneously. Finally, Watch-to-Earn (W2E) capitalizes on the popularity of online content consumption, offering viewers opportunities to earn cryptocurrency while watching videos or ads or participating in live streams. Content creators and audiences alike can now benefit from their online engagement.

The growing popularity of X2E strategies can be attributed to several key factors. Of course, one of the primary drivers is the opportunity to gain financial rewards. As the value and recognition of cryptocurrencies have surged, more people are drawn to the idea of accumulating digital assets through various activities. Stories of individuals earning substantial amounts of cryptocurrency through X2E strategies have also generated curiosity and enthusiasm.

X2E platforms have made cryptocurrency accessible to a broader audience. They don't require users to have advanced knowledge of blockchain technology or complex trading procedures; instead, they offer user-friendly interfaces and straightforward mechanisms for earning crypto. This accessibility lowers barriers to entry, making it appealing to both newcomers and experienced crypto enthusiasts.

Many X2E platforms also incorporate social and community elements where users can connect with like-minded individuals, join guilds or collaborate on quests. This fosters user retention and engagement, contributing to the platforms' growth. Advancements in blockchain technology have made X2E strategies more efficient, secure and scalable, enhancing the user experience and enabling platforms to handle a growing user base.

Other than these factors, each of the X2E strategies capitalizes on existing trends, such as the popularity of online gaming. Move-to-Earn strategies align with the increasing focus on health and wellness. Wearable devices and fitness apps have become mainstream, making it convenient for individuals to track their physical activity. In 2016, the number of smart wearable shipments worldwide was 37 million. In 2023, the total was 305 million and by 2026 it's expected to reach 402 million (Statista, 2024). Also, the global wearable fitness tracker market is expected to be worth $30,922.1 million in 2024, reaching $133,218.4 million by 2034 (Yahoo Finance, 2023). What's more, research by Ericsson showed that two in five users of wearables said they felt naked when not wearing their device, with 25 per cent even keeping it on while sleeping (Ericsson, 2016).

It stands to reason that this will translate to increasing interest in M2E. Integration of cryptocurrency rewards for meeting fitness goals provides extra motivation for users to maintain active lifestyles; as such, it may encourage non-users to purchase wearables and take part in M2E strategies. Likewise, Learn-to-Earn platforms have capitalized on the growing demand for online education. Many individuals seek to expand their knowledge and skills and the prospect of earning cryptocurrency while learning serves as an added potent incentive.

Watch-to-Earn platforms leverage the growing trend of online content consumption. Due to the rise in video streaming and social media platforms, people spend a great deal of time watching content. The worldwide average media consumption time is 455 minutes per day, while Gen Z spend an average of 4 hours and 15 minutes per day on mobile devices. In addition, 87 per cent of US households are subscribed to at least one video-streaming service (Lindner, 2023).

Conclusion

While there are regulatory and other obstacles between the current state of things and the widespread adoption of decentralization, the shifting landscape of consumer attitudes, preferences and expectations is undeniably propelling things forward.

In this chapter we have explored several key trends that are shaping the future and influencing how individuals interact with digital platforms. The era of Web 2.0 placed trust in established brands and corporations, but the rise of decentralized technologies is shifting trust from centralized entities to code and communities.

DeSoc is an overarching concept encompassing decentralized governance, finance, communication and production. Decentralized production promotes transparency, efficiency and sustainability in supply chains, benefiting both consumers and the environment, while decentralized communication platforms offer users greater control over their content consumption, eliminating some of the ethical issues traditional social platforms bring to the table. Gen Z are expected to be one of the keys to DeFi and cryptocurrency adoption. Decentralization is also giving people more power to support movements that matter to them, as well as support content creators through micropayments.

Other trends discussed include the tokenization of real-world assets, which democratizes investment and enhances liquidity, while X2E strategies are growing in alignment with existing trends (content consumption, e-learning, etc.).

Some core human behaviours, such as the need for community, safety, trust, happiness and health, remain constant. These factors will continue to play a vital role in consumer decisions, even as Web 3.0 transforms digital interactions. As we navigate this transition, the balance between trust in code, community governance and individual values will therefore shape the future of the internet and our digital experiences.

Notes

Amnesty International (2023) Driven into darkness: How TikTok's 'For You' feed encourages self-harm and suicidal ideation. 7 November, www.amnesty.org/en/documents/POL40/7350/2023/en/ (archived at https://perma.cc/BGP2-9PLM)

Clarke, A (2023) Gen Z and crypto: Will there be a breakthrough in worldwide adoption? Nasdaq. 31 August, www.nasdaq.com/articles/gen-z-and-crypto-will-there-be-a-breakthrough-in-worldwide-adoption (archived at https://perma.cc/5H8N-W3WD)

Ericsson (2016) Wearable technology and the IoT. www.ericsson.com/en/reports-and-papers/consumerlab/reports/wearable-technology-and-the-internet-of-things (archived at https://perma.cc/9L8C-LHEX)

Lindner, J (2023) Must-know media consumption statistics [current data]. 16 December, https://gitnux.org/media-consumption-statistics/ (archived at https://perma.cc/9S74-B8ZW)

Paul, L G (2024) Top 8 Web 3.0 trends and predictions for 2024 and beyond. TechTarget. 17 January, www.techtarget.com/searchcio/tip/Top-Web-30-trends-and-predictions (archived at https://perma.cc/CDM7-RG2B)

Statista (2023) DeFi – Worldwide. www.statista.com/outlook/fmo/digital-assets/defi/worldwide (archived at https://perma.cc/H5Z3-8B4K)

Statista (2024) Smart wearable shipments forecast worldwide from 2016 to 2026. www.statista.com/statistics/878144/worldwide-smart-wristwear-shipments-forecast/ (archived at https://perma.cc/W25F-CEG3)

Upper Echelon (2024) TikTok is digital POISON [YouTube]. www.youtube.com/watch?v=-ihEKWDerlk (archived at https://perma.cc/LVK4-FC7M)

WSJ (2021) Investigation: How TikTok's algorithm figures out your deepest desires. 21 July, www.wsj.com/video/series/inside-tiktoks-highly-secretive-algorithm/investigation-how-tiktok-algorithm-figures-out-your-deepest-desires/6c0c2040-ff25-4827-8528-2bd6612e3796 (archived at https://perma.cc/7538-ZYEP)

Yahoo Finance (2023) Wearable fitness tracker market set to surge, projected reach: US$ 133,218.4 million by 2034 | Future Market Insights, Inc. 23 November, https://finance.yahoo.com/news/wearable-fitness-tracker-market-set-083000184.html#:~:text=Global%20wearable%20fitness%20tracker%20market%20was%20valued%20at%20US%24%2026%2C787.8,share%20of%2043.4%25%20in%202024 (archived at https://perma.cc/E9G6-NDPJ)

17

Building your brand

As we've discussed, many businesses will need to undergo a shift in their brand strategy and how they relate to consumers. People are becoming more discerning about the companies they hand their money over to and are expecting more in return. So, in this chapter we explore how brands can add value in line with changing consumer expectations. Communities are also a fundamental ingredient when it comes to brand strategy in Web 3.0, so I'll also discuss how you can build a meaningful community around your brand – one that's based on shared values and that fosters participation and loyalty.

Establishing how your brand adds value

As I've said, it's going to be increasingly important for brands to stand out. This has been the case for a long time of course, but it is harder now more than ever in a crowded marketplace with such low barriers to entry. However, as we head into Web 3.0, things will step up a notch due to decentralization. Decentralization lowers the barriers to entry even further for new businesses and creators, leading to a more crowded and competitive marketplace. As such, brands need to review the value they're adding already and think about how they can develop on that.

Consumers also have higher expectations than ever. They expect personalization, higher standards of privacy, transparency and userexperience, and they expect to see evidence of corporate social responsibility. As such, brands need to exceed these expectations and offer unique value propositions that resonate with a more discerning audience.

Let's go over each of these expectations and how brands can fulfil them, but first let's take a quick look at the data that clearly demonstrates the demand for this personalized understanding.

According to Salesforce, 73 per cent of customers expect businesses to understand their unique needs and expectations, 62 per cent expect businesses to anticipate their needs and 56 per cent expect offers to always be personalized (Insider Intelligence, 2022). In addition, research by McKinsey revealed that companies implementing personalization generate 40 per cent more revenue. Another survey of marketers in the US and the UK revealed that 33 per cent of respondents were spending more than 50 per cent of their marketing budgets on personalization (Arora et al., 2021; Statista, 2024).

What might personalization look like in practice in the future? Starbucks' Odyssey Loyalty programme, for which testing began in December 2022, is a good example. The programme consists of 'journeys' involving various activities including quizzes and games. Users collect so-called 'Odyssey NFTs' which they can profit from through resale, as well as 'Odyssey points' which unlock other benefits. (Activities include trivia about the company's heritage and a virtual tour of its coffee farm in Costa Rica – another example of the power of immersive brand storytelling.) So, how does personalization come into it? The programme is set up to span extended periods (weeks or months), giving Starbucks the opportunity to collect data that gives insights into customers' habits, informing future rewards. (Some of the higher-level rewards include experiences such as drinks-making classes or visiting Starbucks' farms and roasteries, a prime example of standing out through providing value.) In its own words, the company will 'collaborate with members and partners to co-create the future of the experience'. Some have criticized the programme for being too complex and inaccessible for the average customer compared with those with an active interest in blockchain technologies. Regardless, it's proven to be popular among that segment and it's an optional extension of the existing rewards programme; the remaining customers are not being alienated here (McMillen, 2023; Starbucks, 2022).

In Web 3.0, personalization reaches beyond just addressing consumer preferences. It's about empowering users with control over their data and the content they wish to engage with. Brands that enable consumers to tailor their online experiences according to their own privacy preferences or interests are providing significant value and this can be done through consent-based mechanisms or incentivization. In fact, incentivization may become necessary because consumers will eventually have more control over their data by default, forcing brands to be more creative and increase the value they offer in order to access that data.

Now, let's consider CSR and authenticity. The Web 3.0 consumer places a premium on authenticity and alignment with personal values. The brands that stand out are those that communicate their values transparently and consistently demonstrate them in practice. Again, blockchain makes it possible to provide transparency about sustainable and ethical supply chain practices. This communication of transparency is also effective in industries like finance or real estate, where trust is so fundamental to the business–client relationship.

The expectation for businesses to take an active role in tackling societal issues has implications in terms of data collection. More and more brands are having an impact on areas beyond their own industry. Companies can use this to incentivize customers to share their data – after all, for many people, sharing their data is not much to ask if it helps companies address important issues regarding the environment, public health, inequality and so on.

The technologies emerging with Web 3.0 provide myriad ways to deliver more value to the customer. Again, smart contracts provide a flexible way to share value on collaborative projects such as StoryCo's *The Disco Ball* which I mentioned in the previous chapter. They allow community members to become stakeholders, and the potential to earn through their contributions means greater emotional investment and loyalty in the project, brand and community. Let's consider another (hypothetical) example of how this could work. Suppose a fashion brand wants to create a limited-edition collection with the help of its customers. Each item created could be minted as an NFT (minting is the term for creating a token on the blockchain). These NFTs are then embedded with smart contracts that stipulate the terms for revenue sharing from future sales. This may benefit emerging designers and their communities as the value of the items would increase with time. As such, it becomes a symbiotic relationship in which the community is a contributing factor to the brand's success and the brand's success, in turn, brings in revenue for customers.

Now, NFTs are more than just collectibles; a certain type known as utility NFTs provide their holders with access to specific benefits or utilities beyond mere ownership of a unique digital asset. These benefits can include access to services, products, exclusive content, real-world experiences or rights within a particular ecosystem. They could also be used as proof of membership for clubs and communities. Compared with your average NFT, they are prized for the practical advantages they offer to their owners in digital or physical spaces.

One example is the AMC Spiderman NFT. This was provided for free to customers that pre-purchased tickets with AMC theatres to *Spiderman: No Way Home*. The NFT was linked to a piece of digital art based on Spiderman; when redeeming it, owners could obtain a printed poster of the artwork or download a digital version. Another example is that of identity NFTs, a sub-type of utility NFT that provides a convenient form of identity verification for various services.

Also consider how you can leverage AI in order to deliver more value – both directly to the customer and indirectly through improving your efficiency. In Chapter 9 I discussed the multitude of ways it can help, so let's recap. Generative AI can assist in planning and creating content; of course, when it comes to the types of interactive content I've been discussing, the options are limited, but in terms of text and images it will cut down the workload that comes with producing content at scale. It can also serve as a research assistant and help with strategy development, and AI-powered chatbots greatly save resources while improving the customer experience. AI enables advanced analytics (predictive or otherwise) and assists with segmentation, sentiment analysis and personalization, including the dynamic personalization of email content. It can quickly run thousands of A/B tests for ad copy and speed up the optimization of content for SEO purposes.

AI also helps consumers to shop smarter and not just through personalized recommendations. Again, visual search makes it easier for people to find the products they're looking for, while AI-powered voice assistants enable shopping using voice commands, making the process hands-free and more accessible. Finally, AI-powered pricing optimization is used in several industries, including e-commerce, tourism, hospitality and transport. In e-commerce, for example, algorithms analyse data such as consumer behaviour, competitor pricing, market demand and inventory levels to dynamically adjust prices. There's also personalized pricing based on customer profiles, taking into account factors like their browsing and purchase history.

To sum up, products and services must evolve in line with consumer expectations. There are many ways in which they can develop and provide more value, such as adding decentralized features or introducing AR and VR for product exploration. The goal is to continually reassess and realign your offerings, adapting them as technology develops and expectations change.

Building meaningful communities

Community building is going to be a core business function in the future. Brands that stand out are those that successfully create and nurture online communities, fostering emotional bonds that drive a sense of belonging and loyalty (as well as revenue). There are several key aspects behind Web 3.0 communities: the product or service, a clearly defined brand identity, a team that will develop the community and other collaborators that are driven to work on the project.

Building a community is also about creating a space where individuals feel valued and connected. This means facilitating genuine interactions and providing platforms where users can collaborate, share and grow together. Doing so creates loyal advocates who believe not only in the product but also in the ethos behind it.

It takes a lot of resources to engage with a community non-stop. The good news is, customer-to-customer engagement is the key to building a strong and active community, so it's important to provide platforms for them to interact with each other. Building community spaces that are interoperable across different channels adds further value.

To drive engagement, create immersive shared experiences, collaborative projects and content that sparks conversation. Also, don't underestimate the power of membership. When someone has invested in becoming a member (via emotional investment or taking action), they're more likely to continue investing their time in the community. There's also the element of exclusivity when you're part of something that is somewhat gatekept.

Another crucial point to keep in mind is that communities are based on shared values. Businesses need to identify what values they share with their customers (and by extension, what customers share with each other) and build on that. For example, Tesla appeals to those who value innovation, especially in sustainable technology. Its pioneering electric vehicles and energy solutions symbolize a forward-thinking approach that attracts consumers passionate about technological advancement and environmental sustainability. Nike connects with consumers through empowerment, inspiring people to achieve their athletic best. Its marketing campaigns often focus on overcoming challenges and achieving personal goals, aligning with consumers who value perseverance, confidence and self-improvement. Such values need to be straightforward enough for consumers to easily buy into, but they should still be original. Both of these examples are a perfect illustration of that concept.

It's a human tendency to want to belong to a group or be part of something bigger than oneself. For many people, this is a prime factor in their decision to join a community, while the project itself empowers them to work towards something. That's why it's important to build a community that has a strong, values-based culture.

It's worthwhile spending some time observing other Web 3.0 communities and their cultures and activities. Defining your objectives is also a must. For companies looking to form DAOs, for example, it's going to be more important to find individuals that can invest in them; in other cases, finding influencers and other people that can act as brand ambassadors would be more appropriate to start with. Also, while many communities will be based on blockchain technology, that's not always the case; it's just as important to use the existing channels as well.

Be an early mover or a fast follower

Brands should strive to be early movers or fast followers in the Web 3.0 space. These terms are from the Diffusion of Innovation model, developed by Everett Rogers in 1957. The model seeks to explain how, why and at what rate new ideas and technology spread through cultures. Rogers, a professor of communication studies, popularized this theory in his book *Diffusion of Innovations*, in which he explored the process of adopting innovations over time among a group of participants.

At the heart of the model is the 'innovation', which is any idea, practice or object perceived as new by an individual or other unit of adoption. Early movers take the leap into uncharted territories, setting trends and establishing standards. Fast followers, while not the first, quickly adapt to these new trends, learning from the early movers and improving upon their strategies. Rogers defined three other categories: the early majority, which adopts an innovation after a significantly longer amount of time has passed; the late majority, which adopts an innovation after the average member of the society (these individuals or businesses approach an innovation with a high degree of scepticism); and finally, the laggards – those who are last to adopt an innovation.

The early mover and fast follower approaches have their merits and come with different degrees of risk. Some investors may be more attracted to early movers, for example. Early movers can also have a powerful role in setting industry standards and shaping customer expectations and preferences. In addition, they gain experience and insights ahead of everyone else, allowing them to refine their offerings. Meanwhile, a fast follower may sit back and watch as the early mover makes mistakes, getting ideas for how to do things better; learning from others' mistakes is one way to avoid the risk that comes with experimenting with new technologies and business models. Standing out in a market established by an early mover can be challenging though.

The main thing is to be agile and adapt quickly to new developments. The early majority, while still ahead of the average, may miss the opportunity to be seen as market leaders and they may face limited options for shaping market trends. Finally, by the time the late majority adopts an innovation, the market is likely saturated, leading to intense competition.

Future-proofing your communications

In a rapidly evolving digital world, ensuring that your communication channels are future-proof is crucial. The existing channels are still vital, so don't forget about them. Social media remains an indispensable tool in building your brand, particularly with Gen Z, so keep focusing on providing them with the type of content they prefer, such as short-form TikTok and Instagram content, as well as UGC and challenges. Strengthen your communities on social channels and continue using them to their fullest potential.

In terms of branching out onto new channels, you don't have to immediately create a DAO or start building metaverse worlds on *Roblox* if you don't have the budget or it's not the right time for any other reason. Other platforms that may be new for your brand include Discord, Bluesky and Telegram. Options like these are popular among Web 3.0 consumers. While they offer some of the same features of the other standard social media and communication channels, they provide decentralization and greater privacy. Some of these platforms, such as Discord, are ad-free and do not allow you to collect user data, so the ROI will come in the form of strong community engagement. Discord also enables real-time interaction between members and some businesses use it to host live events.

Conclusion

To summarize, the future of branding is about creating meaningful connections with consumers through innovation, authenticity and a deep understanding of their evolving needs. Doing so is going to be necessary for any business looking to differentiate itself in an increasingly crowded and complex marketplace where consumers have more control than ever over their interactions with businesses, their data and the content they engage with.

Look at how you can provide more value to your audience. This could involve introducing further personalization, making them stakeholders in projects, giving them genuine incentives for sharing their data and so on. Regardless, building strong communities should be a key focus for any brand going forward as this will be the cornerstone of loyalty and advocacy. And remember not to neglect your current channels while embracing new ones. Finally, be an early mover or am fast follower (each has its benefits), but most importantly: don't lag behind.

Notes

Arora, N, Ensslen, D, Fiedler, L, Liu, W W, Robinson, K, Stein, E and Schüler, G (2021) The value of getting personalization right—or wrong—is multiplying. McKinsey. 12 November, www.mckinsey.com/capabilities/growth-marketing-and-sales/our-insights/the-value-of-getting-personalization-right-or-wrong-is-multiplying (archived at https://perma.cc/4KQD-HK9A)

Statista (2024) Share of digital marketing budgets devoted to personalization according to marketers in the United States and the United Kingdom as of February 2020. Statista. 6 January, www.statista.com/statistics/1208559/marketing-personalization-budget-share/ (archived at https://perma.cc/X24J-53EJ)

Insider Intelligence (2022) Attitudes of consumers worldwide toward personalization and customer experience provided by a company, 2020 & 2022. 13 May, www.insiderintelligence.com/chart/256614/Attitude-of-Consumers-Worldwide-Toward-Personalization-Customer-Experience-Provided-by-Company-2020-2022-of-respondents (archived at https://perma.cc/7AXD-9NW5)

McMillen, J (2023) Starbucks Odyssey gives reward NFTs. Will coffee drinkers care? Forbes. 3 October, www.forbes.com/sites/jennmcmillen/2023/10/03/starbucks-odyssey-gives-reward-nfts-will-coffee-drinkers-care/ (archived at https://perma.cc/7AXD-9NW5)

Starbucks (2022) The Starbucks Odyssey begins. 8 December, https://stories.starbucks.com/stories/2022/the-starbucks-odyssey-begins/ (archived at https://perma.cc/YW5A-8ALR)

18

Creating immersive experiences

In this book we have touched many times on the importance of creating experiences that resonate with your audience and represent your brand. Now we turn to how to effectively deliver this and take a look at some nice work already happening in this space that may inspire you.

When I talk about an immersive experience, I refer to one in which the individual is not just touching a brand while on another journey (browsing the internet, walking through a shopping mall or streaming a movie) but where they are fully involved, surrounded and embedded in the experience. One where the experience is taking the user's full attention. This is, of course, best envisioned as a VR experience but is not necessarily reliant on VR technology.

Unlike passive advertisements or static web pages, immersive brand experiences invite consumers into a rich, interactive world where the narrative may unfold in real-time. These experiences go beyond the visuals and messages of current marketing and create an environment where engagement in its truest form is a measure of success. This can build a real sense of loyalty, a deep connection with and understanding of the brand and the moment of joy in association with that brand.

Before you start to create

Having a vision for this and working with a strategic marketing agency (such as my agency, SK) to build something meaningful and brand-aligned is essential. But, as with any good strategy, you must ensure you build up from the foundations. While you may know how to do this with your eyes closed when it comes to established channels, it is worth revisiting this with a specific eye on these immersive experiences.

Understand your audience

You likely already have a grip on your audience. You may know who your customers are, where they live, what their passions are, their income, education and more in terms of demographics and behaviours. None of this, however, tells us what games they play or are aware of. What games do their children play (and therefore your customers are familiar with)? What other technology do they use that would give them an intuitive understanding of how to be involved in your experience?

Coupling this understanding of technology and lifestyle with their passions and your brand is where your brainstorming for ideas should begin. You must bring together your brand values and your audience's passions in an environment that, although new, feels familiar to them. This is the best way of telling your story and removing the psychological barriers of embracing a new technology.

Storytelling is the foundation

Consider your story. What is this experience doing? Is it here to entertain or to teach? Is it going to take the individual on a short adventure where they can win a prize (virtual or physical)? Will it be a short experience that is highly viral or an experience that you want users to return to over the long term?

Based on these sorts of questions you can consider the story. You may wish to get your customers to compete to be the best at a task related to your products (Nike's many uses of VR) or to work together in teams to build an enjoyable world that relies on your products (LEGO *Fortnite*).

Define success

As with everything we do in marketing, it's vital not to get carried away and create something beautiful and experimental for the sake of it – we must focus on contributing towards our goals.

Keep your marketing and business strategy in mind. Why are you creating an immersive experience? Are you looking to deepen your relationship with a certain demographic, build long-term brand loyalty, sell more product or surface your content to a new audience? Whatever your goal, everything you construct should be directed at fulfilling this and you should therefore avoid any development time and budget that distracts from this.

CASE STUDY

FNAC

FNAC is a leading French retail chain specializing in the sale of electronic, technological and cultural products, such as books and music, offering an enriching shopping experience where commerce, culture and technology converge.

Objectives

Some of the biggest retailers are exploring gaming as a marketing tool to reach new generations, which comes with its own playbook and language. FNAC aimed to celebrate the 30th anniversary of the first store in Spain by engaging with the gaming community in a memorable way.

The objective was to develop a marketing campaign that not only showcased the brand but also resonated with gamers, particularly those within the influential Gen Z demographic. *Fortnite* was selected as the platform for the campaign due to its massive reach and popularity among the target demographic. With over 240 million monthly players, *Fortnite* provided an ideal environment to engage with gamers and amplify FNAC's brand presence.

Campaign concept

To achieve its goals, FNAC envisioned creating a unique experience within *Fortnite*. DeuSens meticulously crafted an island within *Fortnite*, divided into zones representing different sections of FNAC stores. These zones featured products like books, music equipment, home appliances and gaming consoles, providing a thematic journey for players.

Activation

Activated on 28 October, this parkour experience, inspired by FNAC store designs, revolutionized *Fortnite*'s creative possibilities. Players explore sections featuring FNAC products, enhancing engagement and brand interaction. To distribute and promote the world, the brand used specialized *Fortnite* streamers, including SujaGG, Miguelillo_RL, Dutygameplays, MateoZ and RecuerdOp, to explore the 'Only Up game,' praising its design and difficulty. Their involvement amplified the campaign's visibility and engagement within the gaming community.

Results

Sara Vega, FNAC's Director of Marketing and Communication, emphasizes the company's commitment to innovation and adaptation to new trends, particularly targeting younger demographics. The positive response by the gaming community reflects the collaboration between FNAC and DeuSens as a success and shows the power of creating unique experiences that transcend physical boundaries, merging culture and technology.

   In addition, Álvaro Antoñanzas, cofounder of the development studio DeuSens, found this project challenging and rewarding. He expressed enthusiasm for the opportunity to merge FNAC's brand identity with the dynamic world of *Fortnite*, highlighting the creative freedom and technical intricacies involved in bringing the 'Only Up' campaign to life. Antoñanzas emphasized the collaborative efforts between FNAC and DeuSens, underscoring the dedication to delivering an immersive and memorable experience for gamers.

Conclusion

FNAC's *Fortnite* collaboration successfully achieved its objectives of celebrating the brand's anniversary while strengthening its connection with the gaming community. By leveraging the popularity of *Fortnite* and working with skilled developers like DeuSens, FNAC created a memorable brand experience that extended its reach to new audiences and showcased its commitment to innovation.

This collaboration showcases the ability of the studio to innovate and engage with audiences through immersive experiences, solidifying brands' position as disruptors in the digital age.

Technology

We have looked at the technology requirements for Web3 in Chapter 5 and we must keep this maturity in mind when building these experiences. If we control the environment where users can interact, e.g. making the experience unique to our physical stores, then we can control the technology and ensure the experience is as we envisioned. If, however, we are enabling users to immerse themselves in our experience en masse, we need to let them do so at home. Once we go into the home environment, there are many variables we need to consider to ensure that what we created is not frustrating for users and the quality does not degrade.

If we partner with an existing game such as *Fortnite* or *Minecraft*, we can have some certainty that the quality (assuming thorough cooperative testing) will be high and users will be on a platform that is already capable of bringing our experience to life. If, however, we create our own experience for PC, there may be issues with the capability of a user's PC (for which there are millions of variants), their internet connection and many other factors (even down to whether their mouse has an issue that the user can't afford to fix).

We cannot account for every eventuality of course, but that is exactly why we must consider who our audience is and therefore how they will experience our initiative.

The future

There is a lot more to come and brands should be consider now how they can build immersive experiences into their strategy for the next few years. To be clear, this is not something to plan to implement in five years, this is something to look at with some immediacy so as not to get left behind by those who are already pushing out fantastic experiences.

Looking ahead, the fusion of AI and immersive experiences is set to reconfigure the landscape further. For example, virtual stores where AI assistants not only guide you through the products but also provide personalized recommendations based on nuanced interpretations of your reactions and responses. Being able to virtually try on clothes at home or in-store is an obvious use, but also eating virtually at a restaurant before you dine in the physical setting.

Conclusion

Immersive brand experiences are the frontier of digital storytelling and the next step in community marketing. Companies willing to embrace this technology stand to gain not just customers but advocates – witnesses to a brand's ability to not just sell a product or a service but invite them into a story worth telling and retelling. As these virtual landscapes evolve, one thing remains certain: the story has just begun.

19

Combining the virtual and the physical

The integration of virtual and physical gives businesses the chance to offer new experiences that were not possible before – experiences that are not only more immersive but also more convenient and enriching. I have mentioned a few examples in previous chapters. To recap, I spoke about how fashion brands are using AR dressing rooms to allow customers to virtually try on complementary products or test items of clothing in different colours and so on, as well as being able to order items there and then. This blend creates more value for customers by bringing them more convenience and saving time, while retailers benefit from additional sales. We also looked at AR in print advertising, where a smartphone brings ads to life, providing additional content and interactive experiences. In this chapter I'll talk about some more real and hypothetical examples of combining virtual and physical elements.

The benefits of physical–virtual integration

Digital omnipresence is a given these days and more companies will start creating immersive experiences. Therefore, merging the virtual and physical is another way for brands to differentiate themselves, the novelty causing word to spread.

Real-world integration is beneficial in terms of educating consumers on a business's value proposition. Companies are using this tactic to create a buzz around product launches, for example, where customers attend physical launch parties and experience the product's features and benefits through interactive holograms and storytelling via VR and AR. Allowing customers to interact with products in a natural and contextual way not only leaves a lasting impression, it can lead to increased product awareness and sales. In addition, users may be more likely to engage for longer durations because such experiences offer both entertainment and functionality.

While standard VR experiences excel in providing fully immersive, purely virtual environments, virtual–physical experiences offer a bridge between the digital and physical worlds, allowing for more practical, context-aware and socially engaging interactions. This connection to the physical world can provide a more relevant and contextualized interaction, as mentioned. Users can then apply what they experience in the virtual space to their real-life situations, making the experience more meaningful. Research by Capgemini reveals that 69 per cent of consumers believe that immersive experiences will lead to them making more purchases online, while 77 per cent agree that such experiences will help them make better purchase decisions. This is also beneficial in terms of sustainability in e-commerce; satisfaction with purchases means lower return rates and therefore fewer transportation miles and less landfill use (Capgemini, 2022).

Many virtual–physical experiences leverage natural user interfaces, such as gesture recognition, voice commands and spatial tracking, making them more intuitive and user-friendly compared with standard VR setups.

On the whole, integrating both elements lets marketers craft multi-dimensional campaigns that leverage the strengths of both realms – the vast reach and analytics capabilities of the digital world combined with the tangibility and human touch of the physical.

Hybrid events

Hybrid events grew in popularity during the pandemic. While they were a necessity at the time, they also demonstrated various benefits. One of their most compelling advantages is their ability to transcend geographical boundaries and reach a global audience. This expanded accessibility is particularly beneficial for international conferences, product launches or cultural events, where participants can engage from anywhere in the world, eliminating the constraints of travel and time.

Of course, allowing people to access an event online using a standard platform is not particularly immersive, but things have developed further. Hybrid event software allows businesses to create events where attendees can join via VR and interact and participate as if they were there for real. (Not all users need to use VR – they can still attend remotely in a more traditional way if they prefer.) Other features include 360-degree views of the venue and virtual networking lounges.

The incentive for companies to develop such experiences is not just engagement but also to increase attendance and in turn, ROI. The additional options a hybrid experience offers makes the event more appealing for people that cannot attend physically; it may also encourage those that are on the fence about whether or not they want to attend.

The virtual restaurant experience

An intriguing application of physical–virtual integration is the concept of a virtual restaurant experience, but not the same type of virtual restaurant you'd find in the metaverse. Instead, this innovative approach would allow customers to enjoy a meal from their home while immersed in a virtual reality setting that replicates eating out at a restaurant. Through VR, they could be virtually transported to a variety of settings, from a cozy Parisian café to a bustling New York pizzeria. Why would someone want to do that instead of just go to a restaurant, you might ask. The key is that this approach lets diners enjoy a meal with friends, family or perhaps clients who are physically elsewhere, creating a sense of togetherness and shared experience despite the physical distance.

Such ideas are merely emerging at the moment. However, some restaurants are actively experimenting with VR, such as the Frenessì Restaurant in Bogota, Colombia. The restaurant is known for offering a unique three-hour immersive dining experience, where customers experience various virtual environments, such as Antarctica or a tropical beach, and the food served corresponds with the environment. Similar experiences are available in Ibiza and, of course, Tokyo (among other locations).

Some other less futuristic but equally valuable experiences provided by restaurants include Wahaca's AR menu. The UK's Mexican restaurant group created the AR experience in order to bring the cuisine to life and provide customers with additional information. Customers scan a QR code on the menu, after which a 3D model of Thomasina Miers, the company's co-founder, appears and guides them through the experience. They can select different sections of the menu and view additional information about dishes, including ingredients and allergens, and information on Wahaca's values, including its sustainability practices and social impact. The integration of a digital payment system linked to the AR menu further streamlines the dining experience, making it more convenient for customers.

Domino's also launched an AR experience called 'New Pizza Chef' allowing customers to use the app to create their ideal pizza. They select the crust and sauce, drag and drop ingredients onto it and preview the final outcome before ordering – the ultimate personalization. After all, the company stated that there are billions of possible combinations, so why confine customers to the limits of the standard menu? Domino's wanted the images to be as life-like as possible so that the final product closely resembled the one created in the app. It also made sure the ingredients shown reflected the actual weight used, which ensured that orders matched customer expectations. Other details included animated characters to enhance the experience. Integrating the experience with the app made things more convenient in case customers wanted to revert to the standard menu, view current deals, track their order and so on. The chief marketing officer spoke about 'the placing of the order through the customer's eyes' – thinking from the customer's perspective should be the starting point for any innovation (Domino's, 2018).

Integrated brand experiences

Now for a couple of case studies where companies have used these technologies to tell their brand's story. Jack Daniels has used AR for such purposes. To promote its partnership with the UK's bar and restaurant chain Slug and Lettuce, the company created an AR experience that came with every glass of Lynchburg lemonade. Customers who ordered the drink could scan a QR code and virtually visit Jack Daniels' distillery in Tennessee. They could explore the facility, discover how their whiskey is made and dress up as the company founder. The company also created an experience where, on pointing their phone camera at a bottle of the whiskey, the label unfolds and guides customers through an animated depiction of the distillery and whiskey-making process, as well as the story of Jack Daniels.

Pepsi used AR for brand awareness purposes during its so-called 'Unbelievable Bus Shelter' campaign in London. AR was used to depict unusual scenes on a digital screen that looked transparent. The scenes included alien invasions and giant robots. The campaign went viral, receiving more than 8 million views on YouTube, of which 3 million occurred during the first five days. In addition, the campaign received international coverage in the media and ultimately reached more than 385 million people. It's safe to say it did a good job of keeping the brand in the forefront of customers' minds (Grand Visual, 2024).

Next, an example of using VR to show customers the real-world impacts of a company's humanitarian efforts. The shoe brand TOMS created an experience centred around the practice of donating one pair of shoes for every sale. In-store, customers enter a VR experience where they can virtually attend a shoe-donating trip alongside the staff. The customer watches children receiving the shoes and their excited reactions, while observing their surroundings and living conditions. This reinforces how TOMS is making a difference while creating an emotional connection with the customer. The company said that reactions to the campaign were extremely positive and very emotional.

A few more examples

Now let's go over a few more examples, real and hypothetical. The tourism industry is another that's ripe for such innovations. Imagine a virtual–physical travel hub where users can physically gather at a travel agency while virtually exploring and booking destinations worldwide. Users could don VR headsets to take virtual tours of their chosen destinations or attend destination-specific events, all while physically interacting with travel experts and fellow travellers. (This could be the key to bringing back the brick-and-mortar travel agent, which has become less relevant as online bookings dominate.) Wellness brands could organize retreats where participants attend physical retreat locations for activities like yoga and meditation but use VR headsets for guided mindfulness sessions, immersive nature experiences and stress-reduction techniques.

Most agree that VR tourism will never replace real tourism (a paper on VR and space tourism states that 87 per cent of survey respondents agree with this sentiment) (Roman et al., 2022). However, it opens up possibilities of visiting destinations that are restricted, dangerous or difficult to visit for economic reasons. The same survey also revealed that many people would like to visit destinations such as North Korea, Syria and Antarctica. In other cases, perhaps people would like to visit virtually a destination that requires a visa, so they can decide whether they'd like to invest in the visa application process and book a trip there in person. VR tourism also enables those with disabilities to visit sites that would otherwise be difficult to access.

There's also the possibility of VR democratizing space tourism in the future. Most people don't have a spare £250,000 for a ticket with Virgin Galactic. However, the option to visit space virtually – in a way that closely simulates the real thing – is an opportunity that many would like to experience. Taking things a step further, how about simulating Mars colonization? There are already games such as 'Surviving Mars' and platforms where users can immerse themselves in the Martian environment. Some suggest this could help prepare future generations if we ever needed to colonize Mars.

Theme parks integrate these technologies to let customers preview rides before trying out the real thing. This is beneficial for those who aren't sure whether they really want to experience it for real, while making adrenaline junkies keen to test it out in person. An example is Cedar Point, a theme park in Ohio that has 72 rides and introduced Valravn, an extreme ride that broke 10 world records, including the fastest dive (75 mph) and longest drop (223 feet).

Similar to the concept of AR changing rooms, brands in the fashion or retail industry could offer AR shopping assistants. Customers would wear AR glasses or use AR apps to receive personalized shopping guidance, outfit suggestions and real-time pricing and availability information while browsing physical stores. If you recall, I mentioned using AR to enhance the experience at events using elements such as virtual maps, augmented signage and gamified experiences. Well, American Apparel used this approach in-store, setting up a personalized navigation system that guided customers to specific items and provided product information. Its app also uses AR to bring the convenience of online shopping to physical stores, allowing customers to scan items and view product variations, reviews and so on – much like viewing an actual web page. Research by Retail Perceptions shows that 61 per cent of consumers would choose to shop in a store that offers AR compared with one that doesn't (Balistreri, 2022).

In fact, Capgemini's research indicates that retail is the industry with the highest consumer demand for metaverse experiences, followed closely by organizations selling products such as cars, furniture and household electronics (Capgemini, 2022).

Real estate agencies can benefit greatly from integrating VR and AR into their marketing process. Goldman Sachs predicts that around 1.4 million real estate agents will use VR and AR by 2025 (Goldman

Sachs, 2016). Agents can provide virtual–physical tours of properties. Prospective buyers visit the physical location but use AR or VR to visualize interior designs (as with the IKEA Place app) or how the property might look at different times of the day or year. It's also helpful when presenting unfurnished properties and developers could even partner with interior design companies to sell the furniture and designs demonstrated using AR. Likewise, virtual tours help with marketing properties that are yet to be built.

Another possibility is to help potential buyers visualize more extensive renovations such as extensions. Some companies use architectural visualization, setting up showrooms with models of different properties which can be augmented with AR and VR. This is efficient in that buyers can view numerous properties in one location, saving both them and the agents a lot of time. VR and AR solutions can also help landlords and tenants work together to resolve problems in their properties, using virtual instructions.

Museums, cultural institutions or heritage sites can offer immersive experiences where visitors physically explore historical sites or exhibits while AR and VR technologies provide historical context, interactive narratives and visual reconstructions of ancient civilizations. Likewise, educational institutions could establish mixed-reality learning centres that combine physical classrooms with virtual experiences. Students physically attend classes but use AR or VR technology for immersive historical reenactments, science experiments or interactive simulations that complement their learning. This integration can also be used for educational marketing, delivering interactive product tutorials, how-to guides and informative content.

Art galleries could augment works of art with VR experiences. Imagine walking through a surreal Dalí piece, for example. Such experiences would likely generate much more interest in art among those that otherwise might not be keen and this brings up an important point. These new technologies have the power to expand a business's reach to new audiences by providing enriching experiences that add value to their lives.

In Chapter 8 I mentioned Volvo's mixed reality showroom; Toyota offers a similar experience where visitors can customize prospective cars and view different configurations. Overall, being more informed through this rigorous exploration can enhance customer satisfaction as they gain more certainty about their purchase before committing. Toyota also provides AR experiences online where customers can carry out similar modifications via ads and other online media, and a VR showroom that provides 360-degree views of the interior and exterior of the vehicles.

Conclusion

The integration of virtual and physical experiences is revolutionizing the way businesses engage with customers and create value. As discussed throughout this chapter, the benefits of combining virtual and physical elements are substantial, from differentiation to greater satisfaction with purchases to greater sustainability. The possibilities to design integrated experiences are endless and businesses have more potential than ever to create engaging, meaningful and valuable experiences that convert and build customer loyalty. As technology continues to advance, we can expect to see many more innovative experiences that bridge the gap between the virtual and physical worlds.

Notes

Balistreri, E (2022) 15 statistics every executive should know about AR MR & VR, goHere AR. February 18, www.mixyourreality.com/articles/15-statistics-every-executive-should-know-about-ar-mr-vr (archived at https://perma.cc/KE86-DMBK)

Capgemini (2022) Total immersion. https://prod.ucwe.capgemini.com/wp-content/uploads/2022/12/CRI_Immersive-Experiences.pdf (archived at https://perma.cc/852P-4BEU)

Domino's (2018) Domino's launches world's first augmented reality pizza chef (Anz). https://investors.dominos.com.au/news/2018/11/22/dominos-launches-worlds-first-augmented-reality-ar-pizza-chef#:~:text=The%20latest%20in%20the%20Company's,app%20on%20their%20mobile%20device (archived at https://perma.cc/EXE5-VWQS)

Goldman Sachs (2016) Virtual and augmented reality. www.goldmansachs.com/intelligence/pages/technology-driving-innovation-folder/virtual-and-augmented-reality/report.pdf (archived at https://perma.cc/LV6V-HEEK)

Grand Visual (2024) Unbelievable bus shelter. https://grandvisual.com/work/pepsi-max-bus-shelter/ (archived at https://perma.cc/ZK5E-GNVR)

Roman, M, Kosiński, R, Bhatta, K, Niedziółka, A and Krasnodębski, A (2022) Virtual and space tourism as new trends in travelling at the time of the COVID-19 pandemic. *Organizacao Mundial da Saude*. 14(2): 628, November. https://pesquisa.bvsalud.org/global-literature-on-novel-coronavirus-2019-ncov/resource/pt/covidwho-1613971 (archived at https://perma.cc/4WZ6-8UGA)

20

Building your marketing team in Web 3.0

Marketers are facing the challenge of adapting their teams to reflect the demands of Web 3.0. Many roles will require a fusion of innovative and creative thinking, combined with technical know-how. In this chapter I give an overview of some of the emerging roles to be aware of and some tips for building these new teams. Also note that since data analysis is becoming more and more critical across the board, some existing roles will evolve and require analytical skills when they didn't before. Companies working with data to a more rigorous extent may decide to employ dedicated specialists to handle such tasks and guide their strategy. The scope of different roles will change with time and vary according to the objectives of each business.

AI specialists

Given the unprecedented integration of AI into marketing strategies that we're seeing already, Web 3.0 has generated the need for AI specialists. These individuals are responsible for implementing AI tools to automate and improve marketing strategies. They may work closely with data analysts, acting on the insights they uncover. For example, consider the need to personalize a campaign. Based on the insights gained through data analysis, AI specialists develop personalized experiences using techniques such as dynamic email marketing.

They also implement AI to automate repetitive tasks such as installing chatbots and improving their utility over time.

To excel as an AI specialist, one must have a deep understanding of how to use AI technologies and get the most out of them. After all, while AI provides insights, it takes a creative mind to translate these insights into compelling marketing campaigns. These specialists possess the creativity to develop unique and engaging strategies that resonate with target audiences. It's also important that they can communicate with technical and creative individuals – for example, they need to translate technical concepts for creative teams and explain business needs to engineers and data scientists. In some cases, they will work alongside data scientists to refine AI models, so a deep understanding of how these models work is advantageous.

Another facet of the role is using generative AI to develop content. As such, proficiency in AI-powered content-generation tools and platforms is essential, including text and image generators. With that said, it's essential that they adhere to a strong quality-control process, which includes reviewing and editing AI content to ensure it aligns with the brand's voice and quality standards. They must also be aware of the ethical implications of using AI in this way, including issues related to plagiarism, misinformation and bias, and should be vigilant in ensuring content adheres to ethical guidelines.

Creativity remains a cornerstone of content creation, even when AI is involved, so these professionals must adapt their creative thinking to work in tandem with AI, leveraging it to enhance their content rather than replace their creative input.

The world of AI is in constant state of flux, with new tools and platforms emerging regularly. AI specialists must be highly adaptable, continuously learning and staying on top of the latest advancements in order to remain effective in their roles.

Content strategists

Web 3.0 has transformed content creation from a simple act of producing material to a more complex role that intertwines creativity, technological know-how and a deep understanding of decentralized platforms. Content creators in this era are not just writers, videographers or artists, they are storytellers who must weave narratives that resonate with a digital audience that values authenticity, interactivity and personalization. This evolution requires creators to have a thorough understanding of how new technologies such as blockchain, AR and VR apply in the context of marketing.

Content quality and storytelling are more important than ever. With the overload of information available online, only the most compelling and well-crafted content stands out. Creators must therefore focus on producing high-quality, engaging and informative content that tells a story. This storytelling is not just about relaying information, it's about creating an emotional connection with the audience.

Content strategists must adapt their strategies to decentralized platforms, which often have different algorithms, audience behaviours and engagement metrics compared with traditional platforms. Understanding these nuances is crucial in effectively reaching and engaging with audiences in a decentralized digital world.

Experience designers

As you know, Web 3.0 marketing is about more than just selling products or services, it's about creating memorable and emotionally resonant experiences for customers. Experience designers play a pivotal role in this process by orchestrating a series of interactions and touchpoints that leave a lasting impact on consumers. These specialists understand that in today's digitally connected world, customers crave authentic and engaging experiences that resonate with them on a personal level. As a result, experience designers are entrusted with the task of crafting and delivering these exceptional customer journeys.

The influence of experience designers is profound and far-reaching. Exceptional experiences drive customer engagement and foster brand loyalty; as such, these experts create interactions that go beyond transactional moments, leaving a positive and lasting impression on customers. They influence content strategies, ensuring that content aligns with the brand's overarching experience, and this includes interactive content, immersive storytelling and user-generated content that enhances the brand narrative.

Experience building is inherently creative. These specialists are known for their ability to think outside the box and design unique and memorable customer touchpoints. They also understand the importance of storytelling and how it can be woven into the brand experience. The experiences crafted by these specialists evoke emotions. Emotionally resonant experiences are more likely to be shared, further amplifying the brand's reach through word of mouth and social media. As such, these professionals should have a good understanding of the emotional effects their content will have. They should also have a deep understanding of the technologies that characterize Web 3.0 – even though many businesses outsource the technical work to agencies or employ developers, to understand the potential of each of these technologies is a must for anyone designing an experience.

While creativity is paramount, data-driven insights guide the work of experience designers. They will either work with data analysts or possess strong analytical skills themselves in order to assess the effectiveness of their strategies, make data-driven refinements and continuously enhance the customer journey.

User experience designers

On a related note, we also need to consider the role of traditional user experience designers (UXDs). When hiring UXDs for Web 3.0 and decentralized applications, marketers should prioritize candidates who not only exhibit strong fundamental skills in UX design but also demonstrate a deep understanding of the unique challenges and opportunities presented by the Web 3.0 ecosystem. Key considerations include familiarity with blockchain technology and decentralized networks. UXDs should be adept at designing intuitive and user-friendly interfaces for complex systems, often involving transactions and interactions that are different from traditional web environments. Experience or a strong interest in cryptocurrency, NFTs and other digital assets is beneficial.

Additionally, given the emphasis on data security and privacy in decentralized platforms, UXDs should be knowledgeable about incorporating privacy-by-design principles and ensuring that user data is handled securely and transparently. Marketers should also look for UXDs who are innovative and adaptable, capable of navigating the rapidly evolving landscape of Web 3.0, and who can design experiences that resonate with a tech-savvy audience while remaining accessible to newcomers in the decentralized space.

VR, AR and metaverse developers

VR, AR and metaverse developers play a pivotal role in marketing teams by actually creating the experiences that have been designed. In many cases, marketers outsource this function to a specialist agency, though some organizations may find it more appropriate to have them in-house.

VR and AR developers specialize in building virtual environments and augmenting real-world experiences with digital overlays. Their work involves designing and programming immersive experiences that can transport users to entirely virtual worlds or enhance their physical surroundings with digital information and interactivity.

Metaverse developers take VR and AR a step further by creating interconnected virtual worlds where users can interact with each other and with the brand in real-time. These developers are skilled in creating spaces within the metaverse where brands can host events, open virtual stores and offer unique experiences that bridge the physical and digital worlds. As such, they should also have a solid understanding of blockchain, given its role in the metaverse, as I've explained before.

These developers are adept at leveraging cutting-edge technologies such as 3D modelling, real-time rendering and interactive design. They work closely with AI specialists, data analysts and content creators to integrate various technologies into a cohesive and engaging user experience. This interdisciplinary approach is crucial in creating seamless and impactful virtual experiences.

VR, AR and metaverse developers must also ensure that virtual interfaces are intuitive, accessible and enjoyable. This requires a deep understanding of UXD and how it translates into virtual and augmented spaces.

Blockchain specialists

Blockchain specialists are going to be vital for marketing teams as decentralized platforms and communities catch on. Their primary responsibility is to understand and implement blockchain applications relevant to marketing, so they must have a deep understanding of decentralized networks, smart contracts and digital assets. They may be responsible for developing tokenization strategies that can create unique customer loyalty programmes, implementing smart contracts to automate and secure digital transactions, leveraging blockchain for supply chain transparency and so on. Decentralized platforms offer new avenues for marketing, so these specialists are pivotal in exploring these platforms for marketing opportunities. They understand the nuances of decentralized social media, decentralized finance and other blockchain-based platforms and can identify innovative ways to engage with audiences on these platforms.

Blockchain specialists also have an educational role within marketing teams. They demystify blockchain technology for other team members, enabling them to understand and embrace its potential. This cross-functional collaboration ensures that the entire marketing team is aligned and can effectively leverage blockchain in their initiatives. Therefore, as with any other technical role, they should have the communication skills that allow them to break down complex concepts for a non-technical audience.

Community managers

As you know, the role of community is fundamental to Web 3.0; in turn, the role of the community manager has gained immense significance. These professionals are instrumental in building and nurturing vibrant communities around a brand or project and they must be proactive. They need to foster the development of authentic connections and thus engagement. As such, they need to know how to facilitate conversations and maintain a sense of belonging and advocacy among members. Remember, authenticity is a cornerstone of Web 3.0 marketing; therefore, community managers ensure that brand interactions are genuine and transparent. (For larger projects, a community management team might be necessary, so someone would need to oversee this team and coordinate their activities.)

Community managers are the bridge between a brand and its customers, so they must have a thorough understanding of the project as well as a genuine interest in blockchain. They must possess excellent interpersonal and communication skills in order to engage with community members effectively, convey the brand's message clearly and quickly defuse potential conflicts in a professional manner.

They may also provide technical support as well as review user-generated content and ensure it's in line with community standards. Other tasks include moderation, reviewing community statistics and reporting them back to management, and gathering member feedback in order to inform product improvements and marketing strategies.

Data analysts

In Web 3.0, data analysts hold a central position in marketing teams, tasked with deciphering complex data landscapes to drive strategic decisions. Their role is pivotal in understanding consumer behaviour, market trends and the effectiveness of marketing campaigns in a highly interconnected and data-rich digital environment.

In Web 3.0, they're not just processing conventional datasets, they're dealing with big data, characterized by its volume, velocity and variety. This includes structured data from traditional databases and unstructured data from sources like social media, IoT devices and blockchain transactions. The ability to harness this data using advanced analytics techniques is essential for extracting actionable insights.

Analysts must be proficient in using a variety of analytical tools and technologies, such as AI and machine learning algorithms, to analyse and interpret this data. They must have a strong foundation in statistical analysis, data mining and predictive modelling. Proficiency in programming languages such as Python or R, and familiarity with database management systems, are also helpful. In addition, they should be adept at using visualization tools to present complex data in an accessible and understandable manner. This skill is vital in communicating insights to other team members and stakeholders.

With the increasing focus on consumer privacy, data analysts must navigate the complexities of data collection and usage ethically. They need to be well versed in data privacy laws and regulations and understand the implications of data handling in a decentralized ecosystem like blockchain. They must also collaborate extensively with other team members or departments. For example, their insights are crucial for content strategists in shaping targeted marketing strategies, for AI specialists in developing personalized customer experiences, and for community managers in understanding and engaging with the audience effectively.

Ultimately, their role is strategic as much as it is technical. Their analyses inform high-level decision-making, guiding the marketing strategy in a direction that is not only data-driven but also aligned with the evolving dynamics of Web 3.0. Their work enables a deeper understanding of customer needs and preferences, leading to more effective and efficient marketing efforts.

The key performance indicators (KPIs) used in marketing are shifting and this is another crucial concept they must understand. Traditionally, marketing efforts were primarily measured through conversion-focused metrics such as sales figures, click-through rates and lead-generation data. However, in Web 3.0 there's a growing emphasis on experience-centric measures. This shift acknowledges the importance of the customer journey and the overall experience in driving long-term brand loyalty and engagement.

Therefore, KPIs are increasingly focused on measuring user engagement, customer satisfaction and the quality of interactions between the brand and its audience. Metrics such as time spent on a website or app, interaction rates with content and customer feedback scores gain prominence. Another way to put it is that KPIs are increasingly focused on measuring long-term value rather than short-term gains. Metrics that reflect customer loyalty, lifetime value and brand advocacy are prioritized. This approach acknowledges that the true measure of marketing success these days is not just in immediate conversions but in building lasting relationships with customers.

With the rise of communities, sentiment analysis becomes an essential tool in understanding brand perception. It's therefore important to focus on KPIs related to social media mentions, tone of customer conversations and overall sentiment. These types of indicators offer deeper insights into how customers perceive and interact with a brand, going beyond mere transactional data.

Also, the new, decentralized platforms come with their own sets of data; analysts need to integrate data from these platforms to gain a comprehensive view of marketing performance. Metrics related to blockchain interactions, NFT engagements or decentralized social media activity become part of the KPI framework, requiring marketing teams to adapt their analysis and reporting methods.

The shift towards a privacy-first approach in Web 3.0 also influences the choice of KPIs. As data privacy becomes a priority for consumers, marketing teams must rely on KPIs that respect user privacy while still providing valuable insights. This shift requires a balance between data collection and consumer privacy, emphasizing the importance of consent-based metrics and anonymized data analysis.

IOT marketing specialists

IoT marketing specialists play a crucial role in crafting personalized, interactive and data-driven campaigns that resonate with target audiences and enhance customer engagement. Their key responsibilities include developing and implementing innovative marketing strategies that leverage IoT technology and working with the insights uncovered by analysts regarding consumer behaviour and campaign effectiveness. They will need to collaborate with development teams to integrate IoT solutions into marketing initiatives as well as ensure all IoT marketing practices comply with data privacy and security regulations.

Naturally, they must have a deep understanding of IoT technology – how various devices connect and communicate with each other and with users. This knowledge is crucial in creating marketing strategies that leverage these interactions (using data from smart home devices to offer tailored product recommendations or utilizing wearable tech for immersive brand experiences). Like virtually all the other roles discussed, they should be able to think creatively and innovatively, developing novel, data-driven solutions. They must have a strong focus on enhancing the customer experience using IoT.

Key considerations when building a team

A core characteristic of a Web 3.0 marketing team is technological proficiency. Team members must be comfortable with emerging technologies and understand how these can be applied to marketing strategies, even if they don't use them as part of their own roles to begin with. As we've seen throughout the preceding chapters, the facets of Web 3.0 are complex and intertwined, so a good general knowledge of the different possibilities is helpful. The interdependent nature of digital marketing requires seamless communication and coordination among various roles, another reason potential team members should be well versed in Web 3.0 technologies, at least at a high level.

Continuous learning and adaptation should be a part of the team culture, enabling members to stay abreast of technological advancements and integrate them into their strategies when it becomes relevant for them to do so. As such, recruiting for a Web 3.0 marketing team involves looking for individuals who are not only skilled but also adaptable and eager to learn. It's also important to create an agile environment where team members can quickly adapt to changes, test new ideas and learn from both successes and failures. Encourage a culture of innovation, where experimentation is valued and creative solutions are sought.

Finally, I'll emphasize the importance of data literacy once again. While data analysts will play a critical role, the team overall should have a strong focus on data-driven decision-making. All team members should be comfortable interpreting data and using insights to guide their strategies.

Conclusion

As we have explored in this chapter, building a marketing team for the Web 3.0 era requires a strategic blend of diverse skills, innovative roles and a forward-thinking approach. The transition from traditional to Web 3.0 marketing is not just about adopting new technologies, it's about embracing a new mindset where flexibility, creativity and customer centricity are at the forefront.

AI specialists and data analysts provide the backbone for data-driven strategies, while experience designers and content creators craft compelling narratives and immersive experiences. Community managers nurture and grow communities, fostering engagement and loyalty and creating brand advocates. Blockchain specialists, with their deep understanding of decentralized technologies, open new avenues for secure and innovative marketing practices, while VR, AR and metaverse developers push the boundaries of customer interaction, creating engaging and memorable brand experiences. IoT marketing specialists also have their unique contribution to bring to the table.

As organizations strive to make their mark in the Web 3.0 world, the composition and capabilities of their marketing teams will be a significant determinant of their success. Integrating these roles into a cohesive team is key to harnessing the full potential of Web 3.0. A culture of continuous learning, adaptability and collaboration is fundamental as the digital landscape is in constant flux.

INDEX

NB: page numbers in *italic* indicate figures or tables

Looking for another book?

Explore our award-winning
books from global business
experts in Marketing and Sales

Scan the code to browse

www.koganpage.com/marketing

More from Kogan Page

ISBN: 9781398602007

ISBN: 9781398610170

ISBN: 9781789666014

ISBN: 9781398605978

www.koganpage.com

From 4 December 2025 the EU Responsible Person (GPSR) is:
eucomply oÜ, Pärnu mnt. 139b – 14, 11317 Tallinn, Estonia
www.eucompliancepartner.com

www.ingramcontent.com/pod-product-compliance
Lightning Source LLC
Chambersburg PA
CBHW070941050326
40689CB00014B/3297